JESUS
AND OUR QUESTIONS

BY
H. MORTIMER SINFIELD
Author of '*The Only Way*'

LONDON
THE EPWORTH PRESS
25-35 CITY ROAD, E.C.1.

First Edition, 1932
Second Edition, 1934
Third Edition, 1935

Made and Printed in Great Britain by
A. BROWN & SONS, LIMITED, HULL.

TO

MY FATHER

WHO LAID THE FOUNDATION OF MY THOUGHT

AND

TO

MY MOTHER

WHO FIRST TAUGHT ME TO LISP THE NAME

WHICH IS ABOVE EVERY NAME

CONTENTS

NOTE

Special permission has been received, and, when necessary, fees paid, for the quotations referred to below, and for which the author desires to express his gratitude.

To Rev. R. J. Campbell, D.D., and Messrs. Ernest Benn & Co. Ltd. for quotation from *The Life of Christ*.

To John Lane, The Bodley Head Ltd. for permission to quote Mr. G. K. Chesterton's words from *Orthodoxy*.

To Mr. H. N. Casson for quotation from *Looking on the Bright Side*.

To the John Murray Press for quotation from A. C. Benson's *The Thread of Gold*, and Bowie's *The Master*.

To Messrs. Constable & Co. Ltd. for quotations from the works of Mr. Bernard Shaw.

To Messrs. Macmillan & Co. Ltd. for quotations from the works of Lord Tennyson.

To Mr. John Masefield for the quotation from *The Everlasting Mercy* (Heineman).

To Messrs Hodder & Stoughton Ltd. for quotations from *The Story of Christ*, by Papini, *What Christ Means to Me*, by Grenfell, and the works of Studdert Kennedy.

To Mr. Channing Pollock & Messrs. Curtis Brown Ltd., for quotation from *The Enemy*.

To Messrs. Harper & Co. for quotation from *The Terrible Meek*, by Charles Rann Kennedy.

To Messrs. A. & C. Black for quotation from Schweitzer's *Primaeval Forest*.

To Mr. Bruce Barton & The Bobbs-Merrill Company for quotations from *What Can a Man Believe?*

To Messrs Longmans Green & Co. Ltd. for quotations from Mr. Studdert Kennedy's *The Word and the Work*.

FOREWORD

THE author of this little book has asked me, as one of his College Tutors, to write a foreword to it. I have much pleasure in doing so, as I think the series of talks contained in it will greatly help the people they are intended for. If some readers are inclined to be critical of their conversational and colloquial style, they should remember the audiences to which they were originally delivered. They appear to me to contain mission-preaching of the best type, and one could forgive a great many more literary blemishes to a preacher who brings his hearers to the feet of his Master every time. The influence of Mr. Studdert Kennedy is very noticeable. I venture to think that, for congregations such as those to which Mr. Sinfield preaches with such effect, he could scarcely follow a better model. Those of us who have watched with special interest Mr. Sinfield's development since he left College wish him God-speed with more than perfunctory heartiness in his difficult task.

J. A. FINDLAY.

DIDSBURY COLLEGE,
    MANCHESTER,
        April, 1932.

PREFACE

MOST of the addresses published in this book have been delivered from the pulpit of the St. George's Road Wesleyan Mission, Hull. They were, of course, originally intended only to be spoken.

When composing these addresses I tried to put myself in the position of young men and women of the office-worker, shop-assistant, and apprentice type, and to grapple with the problems which are likely to puzzle them. My language may not always be 'dignified,' but I have tried to use the language and thought-forms of those for whom the addresses were originally intended. The arguments set forth are not original, and, lest I be accused of stealing other people's ideas, and even their very words, let me admit that I have used other authors freely, and in cases where quotations are not acknowledged it is because the quotations have been copied out while reading (often borrowed books) and the sources forgotten.

I send my little book out into the world with a prayer that it may help many along the difficult Road of Life.

H. MORTIMER SINFIELD.

ST. GEORGE'S ROAD,
　　　HULL, 1932.

'Jesus saith unto him . . .
Follow thou me.'
JOHN xxi. 21.

JESUS AND OUR QUESTIONS

CHAPTER I

JESUS AND GOD

Is There a God?

I'VE often been told that 'Felix kept on walking,'
but I've never heard whether he got there or not ! I
suppose he must have done—provided, of course, that
he wasn't walking in a circle ! If you are walking
in a circle you can get yourself excited, and fuss and
sweat and hurry and keep on till you drop—but
obviously, you won't get anywhere, for the simple
reason that you are just following the same little
orbit over and over again.

There are lots of people who are doing that in life ;
and they usually make a fuss over it, too ! They're
always in a hurry, they are breathlessly busy ; but
they never get anywhere, for the very simple reason
that they are moving in a circle.

If you want to get anywhere you must have a
definite object in view. That's obvious. In other
words, direction determines destination. If you set
out for Liverpool you don't expect to arrive in
London ; if you set out for Worcester you don't expect
to arrive on Wigan Pier ! If you set out for Hell,
you don't expect to arrive in Heaven.

Very few of us, I'm afraid, ever take the trouble to ask ourselves where we are going. Where are YOU going? What are you trying to do with your life? Why was it given to you? What should you strive to be and do? To answer these questions is really to formulate for yourself a *Belief*—to make a *Creed*.

Lots of people in this post-war age will tell you that you can get on quite well without a creed. They say 'it's not your creed, but your conduct that counts!' They'll tell you that it doesn't matter what you believe—it's what you *are* and what you *do* that counts! What does it matter what a man believes so long as he does what is right? You can believe what you like—you can be a Mormon, a Buddhist, a Baptist—whatever you like, so long as you pay your bills, your weekly instalment for the piano, and keep out of the police court. It's *doing* right that matters! That's how we talk, and it all sounds well! But when you come to examine it you recognize it as just undiluted nonsense!

It's doing right that matters! Agreed! But what is right? What ought we to do? We should do our duty! Yes, but what is our duty? 'A man does his duty when he fulfils the purpose of life.' Yes, but what is the purpose of life? An airplane is a good airplane when it flies—that's what it is for! A man is a good man when what? What's he for? To answer these questions is to formulate a belief—to make a creed for yourself. It *does* matter what you believe. Many of the men who were responsible for the Great War were sincerely carrying out their creed. It was their honest belief that turned the world into a shambles. They believed in the Fatherland,

Patriotism, Might is Right, and so on, and their belief cast men into hell. Their creed caused chaos. What you believe matters everything !

But, you say, what can we believe ? The Roman Church teaches one thing, the Protestant Church another. Dr. Barnes tells us one thing, and Dr. Dinsdale T. Young another. The *Methodist Recorder* has one theology and the *Joyful News* another. What are we to believe ? It certainly is very confusing, and you must think the matter out for yourself. All I can do is to suggest a few thoughts that may be helpful.

First. The Apostle's Creed begins like this—' *I believe in God.*' What an assertion ! It's staggering ! God ! Who is God ? What is He ? Where is He ? You can't see Him, hear Him, handle Him ! He seems remote—invisible, intangible, incomprehensible !

Let's begin with something we can understand.

I believe in MYSELF. Ah, now we are in the realm of fact. *I am I.* I feel sure of that ! I can feel myself, hear myself talk, see myself—all but my face (which is a wise dispensation on the part of Providence !). I can bite myself ; taste myself ; weigh and measure myself ; photograph myself, and all kinds of things like that. *I am I.* I'm certain of that.

In a very interesting little book called *What Can A Man Believe* ? Mr. Bruce Barton says, ' The most important discovery I ever made was that when I got my toe into my mouth it was not quite the same as when I got a corner of the blanket of my crib into my mouth. I discovered that my toe was the limit, in that direction, of the thing I was beginning to think of as me. When I got my toe into my mouth, my

mouth gave a feeling of satisfaction and so did the
toe. With the blanket it was different. There was
a great division in the universe, there was Me, and the
things outside Me.' He discovered that He was He,
and different from the things he could see. Tennyson
expresses the same idea in *In Memoriam* :

> The baby new to earth and sky ;
> What time his tender palm is prest
> Against the circle of the breast,
> Has never thought that ' This is I.'

> But as he grows he gathers much,
> And learns the use of ' I ' and ' me,'
> And finds ' I am not what I see,
> And other than the things I touch.'

That is the first article in my creed. I am I.
The second is like unto it—*I am intelligent*. Most
people can say that ! If I tell you, gentle reader,
that you are like a cow, you'll probably feel insulted.
But you are ! I mean, you have two eyes—so has a
cow. You have two ears—so has a cow. You can
walk, eat, drink and sleep—so can a cow. But you
can think of the nasty things you are going to say to
your neighbour the next time you see him, and the
cow can't. In other words, you have that wonderful
thing called intelligence and the cow hasn't. You
can draw up a programme covering weeks or years
and go through with it, foreseeing difficulties and
making provision for the unexpected. Given a
result you can probably play the part of Sherlock
Holmes and reckon back to the causes. And so on.
*I believe that I exist as a separate and intelligent
personality*. Well, then, what use is all that ? It's of

tremendous importance. Unless you believe in yourself you are useless. You must have faith in yourself.
You must believe in your own abilities and your own
possibilities. A man reads a book and he thinks,
' I should like to write a book like this . . . but then
I couldn't—I haven't the ability.' And he stops
there. He's the stick-in-the-mud. Another says, ' I'd
like to write like that—I'll have a try.' And, believing
in himself, his own value, his own possibilities, his
own abilities, he sits down and writes. He may be a
Shakespeare, a Milton, or a Burns—those men believed
in themselves.

Now, in order to make life worth while we must
have faith in ourselves. Perhaps in the past you have
attempted tasks, and failed. Perhaps you've tried
certain business adventures and failed. Perhaps
adversity has come your way and tried to crush
you. Perhaps you've been tempted and failed.
Never mind ! Don't lie down like a wounded
animal and moan and groan and feel sorry for
yourself. Get up ! Pull yourself together. Remind
yourself of what others have done, and remind yourself
of what you *can* do. And then set to work and do it !

Again, *I believe in* LIFE ! I live ! We are sure of
that ! I live !

Now there are two ways of living, just the same as
there are two ways of doing anything. There is the
bad way, and there is the good way. If you are
making a cake you can make it in such a way that
when it's done it will be as hard as a stone and fit only
for paving the garden path. If you are poaching an
egg you can poach it in such a way that when it's
done it will be a thorough mess—a sort of cross between

a blancmange and an oyster ! On the other hand, you can make your cake so soft and delectable that people, like Oliver Twist, will cry out for more ! You can poach your egg so that it is delightfully delicious. So with life. You can live so that life is a thorough mess, like a half-poached egg, so that others will be made miserable, so that often lives will be damned, and so that those who come after you will curse you. On the other hand, you can also live in such a way that others will be made happier, that the world will be made better and brighter, and that those who come after you will reverence your memory, and praise God that you ever existed. Which is the better way ? The answer is obvious.

Well then, we believe in ourselves—our lives, our possibilities, and our own powers of choice. We can now reach out and touch God, the Lord of Life !

I am I. I am intelligent. I live. Who made me ? You evolved, the scientist says. Well then, who invented evolution ? Who set the ball rolling ? Who started it all ? There must be a first cause. If one day as I walk down the street I see a pile of bricks dumped down, the next day a wall being made, the next some scaffolding poles pointing up to heaven, then later some windows in the walls, and later still a roof on the walls, until at last a house appears : even though I've never seen a single man at work I'm not so stupid as to say that house built itself ! I say there is someone behind all that—someone who has planned it, worked out the cost, drawn the plans, placed the bricks, and so on. It may have evolved— I've seen it—but there is an intelligence behind the evolution.

So with the universe. I say, because I have intelligence, there must be intelligence behind the universe. Because otherwise the universe has created something greater than itself, for it has created me. In other words, because *I am*, I believe *God is*. I cannot explain the universe, myself or life without God. I must have God.

Can I prove God? Can I prove Him as I would prove a proposition in Euclid? No I can't. It's an assumption—a working hypothesis—I feel the need of God, I make the assumption and live on it.

' True religion,' Donald Hankey once put it, ' means betting your life that there is a God.' That's what religion works out at really—it's a great venture ! Of one or two things I am certain. There's good and evil in the world, that's certain. Why, I don't know. But this I know—I've got to choose between the two —I must, there's no option : so I choose the good.

As Studdert Kennedy in his poem ' Faith ' says :

> I have to choose. I back the scent of life
> Against its stink. That's what Faith works out at
> Finally. I know not why the Evil,
> I know not why the Good, both mysteries
> Remain unsolved, and both insoluble.
> I know that both are there, the battle set,
> And I must fight on this side or that.
> I can't stand shiv'ring on the bank, I plunge
> Head first. I bet my life on Beauty, Truth,
> And Love . . .
> I bet my life on Christ.

And this brings me to the last point.

I believe in JESUS. I've been talking about God. I feel sure there *is* a God. But what is God like ? We little human beings can never really understand

God because He is too great for us—His brilliance
dazzles us, His magnitude awes us. He is infinite
and we are finite.   He is <u>abstract</u> and we are concrete
—He is the Absolute.   He baffles our understanding
and staggers our imagination.

spiritual?

But I *can* understand Jesus.   And when I turn to
Him I feel that there is in Him all that I would like
to be myself.   When I read of Him I feel like praying
—' I would be like Him, show me the way.'   There
was a sweep and profoundity, a nobility and loftiness
about Jesus such as there has been about no other.
And I believe that God is like Jesus.

You want to argue ?   Well, then argue !   You can
argue for a life-time and it won't help you a great deal.
If you are like me, you'll argue yourself into a belief
and out of it again ; in and out like Cornish villagers
dancing the Floral Dance—in and out of the houses !
You'll become a sort of intellectual gymnast and then
you'll be forced back to this—that life is not so much
an argument as a choice, not a debate but a decision.
All life is choice—you choose foods : and if you
choose the bad you suffer the consequences.   You
choose a wife or husband—and if you choose the wrong
one you get to know about it later !   You choose a
business or profession, and if you choose the wrong
one, then the whole of your life may be blasted.   You
choose a Life Leader—one can lead you to heaven
and another to hell.

Well then, let's apply all this to ourselves.   The
past is past and nothing can alter it.   But the future
is ours.   What about it ?   What's it going to be ?
Are we going to live it as we would live through a
wet Bank Holiday, just looking through the window

and grumbling at the rain, hanging about and doing nothing in particular ? Or are we going to live it as we would live through a battle, struggling and striving, working and scheming for a definite purpose ?

Byron lived the Bank Holiday type of life—and you know the result—exile, desertion by his friends— dejection and despair. He wrote :

> Through life's dull road so dim and dirty,
> I have dragg'd to three-and-thirty.
> What have these years left to me ?
> Nothing—except thirty-three.

That was an aimless, drifting life—the circle-walking business. That was life without God ! But there have been thousands who have lived the better type of life—and we remember them with gratitude, and bless them for the benefits they have bequeathed to civilization. And of this type Jesus was the supreme example.

And that Jesus, once disfigured, shamed and spat upon, comes to us, as someone has said, with death in His bleeding hands and feet, but life in the light of His burning eyes, and demands of each one of us— a choice—a choice between the foul and the fair in life—between good and evil—between hate, selfishness and lust, and unselfishness, integrity and love. He will not go away. He is driving us to a decision with those wounded hands of His.

CHAPTER II

JESUS AND MAN

Is Man as Important as He Thinks He is ?

HAVE you ever thought what a fascination the moon and the stars have—especially for young couples ! There's something about a purple night-sky, sown with its millions of silvery stars that subdues, and makes one tender and romantic ; there's something about the moon and the stars that turns one sentimental, and sometimes makes sensible folk act foolishly. Many a chap has said things in the starlight he would never have thought of saying in the sunlight ; and I would like to suggest (for the benefit of romantic maidens) that you don't believe half of what he whispers to you in the starlight—he'll forget all about it the next day ! It's something in the night air that affects him that way—it goes to his head, like wine.

I wonder if you've ever climbed on to a solitary hill at midnight, and then, away from the ' maddening maze of things ' just gazed into the clear star-spangled sky and let your thoughts run riot ? Standing alone on a hill under a clear midnight sky, the roll of the world eastward is almost a perceptible movement. If you stand perfectly still, fix your eyes on some object and note the position of the stars, in a few minutes you can almost see the panoramic glide of the stars past earthly objects, and if you're camping out in the open and keep looking up into the darkness, you'll see the stars—the Great Bear, the brilliant Sirius, Capella, and the rest of them—swinging round the North Star to the east.

After such a nocturnal reconnoitre it is hard to get back to earth, and to believe that the consciousness of such majestic speeding is derived from a tiny human frame.

David must often have looked at the stars like that. Being a shepherd he'd spend many a solitary night on the hill-side, and he'd know the sky so well that he'd be able to tell the time by the stars' positions. No wonder he put his thoughts into poetry! 'When I survey the heavens, the moon and the stars, what is man?' David saw about 6,000 stars, and, as far as we know, he knew very little about them—he would imagine the sky like an inverted bowl in which were holes through which there shone the light of heaven.

Now, through thousands of years of patient research, our scientists are able even to weigh the stars, to tell us what they are made of, and to measure the distances they are from one another, and from us.

Professor James Jeans, in his amazingly popular book *The Mysterious Universe*, says that most of the stars are so large that hundreds of thousands of earths could be packed inside each and leave room to spare. He says that the total number of stars in the universe is probably something like the total number of grains of sand on all the sea shores of the world. For the most part, each star voyages in splendid isolation, like a ship in an empty ocean.

In a scale model in which stars are ships, the average ship will be well over a million miles from its nearest neighbour.

So you see, really you and I are just very, very small microscopic fragments standing on a grain of sand looking at all the other millions of millions of grains of sand in a universe so great and vast that we cannot possibly imagine how very vast it is.

And the space in which all these stars are travelling is freezing cold with hundreds of degrees of frost, and the stars themselves are so hot that the heat of one of our kitchen fires would be like ice cream in comparison ! It makes you feel a bit queer, doesn't it ? It makes you dizzy—almost sea sick as you think of it !

' When I survey the heavens, the moon and the stars—what is man ? ' . . . In other words, what are you—you miserable microbe ! . . . What am I ? . . . A tiny, infinitesimal, insignificant, unimportant speck in an infinite universe.

It makes you feel a worm, doesn't it ? One of our hymns says something about us human beings being just miserable worms, and any self-respecting person resents being called a worm and refuses to sing the hymn . . . but, when you begin studying astronomy, you soon begin to feel a worm—and a very small, humble little worm, too ! When you smoke your first pipe, or get your first suit of plus fours, or go to your first dance, or see a girl home for the first time—you feel very big and a huge success, but you soon begin to feel small when you think of the stars and sun.

One scientist has suggested that human beings are a disease which has broken out on the earth's surface

—and when you think of those countless blazing white-hot stars in limitless freezingly cold space, you begin to feel something like a disease (at least, I do).

Professor Jeans thinks that human life is just a chemical accident in so vast a universe. ' The utter insignificance of life,' he says, ' would seem to go far towards dispelling any idea that it forms a special interest of the Great Architect of the Universe.' It certainly does make you wonder, doesn't it?

What is man ? If you can pack thousands of earths into one star—like packing thousands of sardines into a packing case—and then have room to spare, why, man is less significant than a speck of dust, an atom, and his life is less important than the wag of a dog's tail.

But, that's only one way of looking at it—that's the purely material way. If you look through a telescope one way things look exceptionally small—but if you turn it round and look through the other end, then things look very different. Let's turn the telescope round.

Professor Jeans thinks that human life is the result of an accident. But, you know, most scientists say that nothing is the result of mere accident—every effect is the result of a cause. A motor-car may skid on a greasy road and run into you and kill you. The newspapers will call it an accident. (Your wife may call it an act of Providence.) But the scientists will say it is cause and effect—the greasy road causes the skid, the skid causes the car to hit you, and the bump puts your light out.

Nothing is purely accidental. If a star suddenly changes colour till it looks like a mouldy bit of cheese, and begins to dance about in the sky like a sailor doing the Horn Pipe, and to make a noise like a girl who has seen a mouse, the scientists will not say it's an accident—they will look as wise as old owls and say, ' there must be a reason for it,' and they'll not rest until they've discovered that reason. Every effect has a cause.

Well then, here we are—worrying, scheming, and puzzling our heads about suns and moons and stars, and Professor Jeans looking through his telescope and writing his books, is with us ! WE, that is, YOU AND I, and Professor Jeans, too, are AN EFFECT. What caused us ?

If you say intelligence, I'm inclined to agree with you. It seems to me that the very fact that Professor Jeans can manipulate a telescope, and work out mathematical problems, and come to conclusions, and write a book about it all, shows that he is greater than anything in the universe that he can see. He may not be great in bulk, but he certainly seems to be in ability—stones and suns and stars cannot think.

Just think how complicated it all is. Professor Jeans peers into a big steel tube in which are arranged several pieces of glass. The result is that he sees stars enlarged until they look as large as footballs. He then sits down in a chair with a pencil—a bit of a tree with some odd material in it which makes marks on some stuff made out of wood-pulp or rags. With this pencil he makes thousands of strange signs or symbols. Then a dirty looking man in his shirt sleeves looks at these signs and puts hundreds of similar signs, made out of lead, into a machine, and then stamps the signs thousands of thousands of times

on to more wood-pulp and rags. And so he produces
that mystery of mysteries, and wonder of wonders—
a book. And then it is sold to me (someone Professor
Jeans has never seen) and I take it up and drink in
through my eyes the ideas which have come into the
Professor's mind as he looked through his telescope.
Then I get ideas, and I get up in a pulpit, and disturb
the atmosphere by the words spoken by my lips,
and thus set up vibrations which beat on the ear-
drums of my congregation and set nerves quivering
and sending messages to a bit of grey stuff in each
skull called ' brain.' And then, by a sudden and
dramatic leap, each listener gets ideas in his mind
similar to those passing through mine. Gracious !
It's a queer business when you come to think of it,
isn't it ?

When one looks into a night sky and thinks of the
vastness of it all it certainly does make one feel small,
but when one turns one's thoughts from stars to self
(particularly one's own intelligence) one begins to
think that it must be the work of a mind AT LEAST
AS GREAT AS OUR OWN.

Look at it this way. (I have borrowed this illustration from Canon Elliott.)

Imagine that I am an artist—one of those queer
fellows with bobbed hair and a big bow. Let me
invite you into my studio. Ah, here we are. By the
window is a large easel, and on it a very lovely picture
of a landscape. You look at it appreciatively, and
then ask if it took long to do it. ' Well, it's a very
curious thing,' I say, ' but I did not paint that picture
at all. Last night I left on the floor of the studio
a blank canvas, and round it were several tubes of

paint. Somehow during the night the cat got in. It put its paws and tail on the paint palette. Why, I can't think—but it did. Then it rolled on the blank canvas and tried to get the paint off. The next morning when I came in after breakfast I found the canvas still on the floor, the paint splashed all over, and on the canvas this picture—curious, isn't it?'

Now, I put it to you—would you believe that? Of course not!

Well, then, here we have the picture—millions of stars in a vast sky, one of them clothed with vegetation—beautiful with mountains and meadows, streams and seas, trees and flowers, sunsets, sweet scents and sweet sounds. The cat couldn't have painted that. It doesn't seem likely that it's just an accident. Most of us would say, 'A mind has been at work'—and a clever mind, too. Why, even Professor Jeans, in the last chapter of his book, suggests that the Great Architect of the Universe is a pure mathematician.

I have been quoting from Sir James Jeans' book *The Mysterious Universe*. It is a very significant fact that three weeks before Christmas, 1930, his book was selling at the rate of 1,000 copies per day. How do you account for the amazing popularity of that book? It's a case of cause and effect again. The book is a 'best seller'—that's the effect. What's the cause? I'll tell you what I think. It is due to the fact that people are anxious to answer the old, old question—WHY? Not only WHY but WHO? . . . Who is it behind this Mysterious Universe? The explanation is at root I think a religious craving. I believe with Canon Elliott, of St. Paul's, that the religious instinct in man is more persistent now than ever it has been in the world's history. Man wants to know—is there a God? . . . Can we know Him? . . . Does He care? . . . Does man count? . . . Is man as important as he thinks he is?

'What is man, that Thou art mindful of him?'
Well, I'm not a scientist. And I'm not a philosopher. I'm just a humble preacher—trying to understand the mysteries of life. And even if I were a scientist or philosopher, it would be utterly impossible for me to do justice to such a subject in a short essay. Whole libraries have been written on it (and still are being written)—and in spite of the fact that so much has been said and written, we are still left guessing. Really all that the scientists and philosophers dare say is, 'It's a mysterious universe.' One scholar says, 'I think this,' and another says, 'I think that.' Sir Oliver Lodge believes in God. Sir Arthur Keith doesn't. To sum up—nobody knows. They're all guessing, or perhaps I ought to say, making assumptions.

And we're just left there. It's like a great game and there's nobody to tell us whether our assumptions are right or not. And it's a very unsatisfactory state of affairs. And you can puzzle till Doomsday—and you won't solve the problem. At least, no one has solved it yet. The Roman Catholics have always been very dogmatic about everything, but they have had to keep retreating step by step as the scientists have driven them from their superstitions. Rome once stated dogmatically that the sun revolved around the earth. That was Truth—the Holy Church *knew*— and to disbelieve it was heresy. But the scientists upset the theory, and so Rome had to climb down and accept the new teaching. The point is that Rome did not know. She is not infallible. No one is infallible—neither the Pope, Professor Jeans, Sir Oliver Lodge, or any one else. We are all assuming.

"Way to God.

Jesus knew --

Meanwhile we're here. 'And we're here because we're here.' And we're alive. (And that's a wonderful thing to say in an age of motors-cars and in cities with slippery streets.) Yes, we're alive. And most of us want to keep alive as long as we can, and we've to find out the best way to do it—in other words, we've to get on with the job of living. And the best way of life, as far as I can see it, is the way of Jesus.

You see, we have reached precisely the same conclusion as we did in the first chapter. After all, there are no final certainties, only tremendous probabilities. You've to make your venture one way or the other ; or, if you use the language of the man-in-the-street, you make your bet. When you say, ' I believe in God the Father Almighty, maker of Heaven and Earth, and in Jesus Christ His only Son Our Lord,' you book your bet. You bet your body, mind and spirit on the great chance. When you puzzle over things as I've been doing in this essay, you are really counting up the odds carefully. And if you refuse to bet because you can't be sure, you are wrong. You've to take risks all through life. If you won't take risks then you won't get married, because your wife may turn out a nagger and a hen-pecker. If you won't take risks you will not play games, because you may break your leg. We must take risks—life consists in making ventures !

So that's where we are—called on to bet on a great tip, and as Studdert Kennedy once pointed out, there's Good and Evil at it hammer and tongs under our very noses, and Life is calling out, ' Roll up. Roll up. . . . Roll up to the great fight. . . . What's the betting, Black or White ? Pay your money and take your chance.'

And to that challenge I say, ' I back White. Back it all out . . . put everything on it. . . . All I've got, talents and time, in fact my whole life—take my life—take everything, and use every power as Thou shalt choose.'

I believe in God the Father Almighty, Maker of Heaven and Earth and in Jesus Christ His only Son Our Lord. I believe that good is finally going to win. I believe that life has a meaning and a purpose. I believe that there is a mind controlling the universe. I call that mind—God. I believe that God is love. I believe that man, though small in stature, does matter. That God loves us as Christ loved us. I believe in Christ and the Christ way of life. ' When I survey the heavens, the moon, and the stars, what is man that Thou art mindful of him ? . . . Thou hast made him a little lower than the angels and crowned him with glory and honour.'

How do I know that God is good ? I don't.
I gamble like a man. I bet my life
Upon one side in life's great war. I must,
I can't stand out. I must take sides. The man
Who is neutral in this fight is not
A man. He's bulk and body without breath,
Cold leg of lamb without mint sauce. A fool.
He makes me sick. Good Lord ! Weak tea ! Cold slops !
I want to live, live out, not wobble through
My life somehow, and then into the dark.

> I must have God. This life's too dull without,
> Too dull for ought but suicide. What's man
> To live for else ? I'd murder someone just to see
> Red blood. I'd drink myself blind drunk,
> And see blue snakes if I could not look up
> To see blue skies, and hear God speaking through the
> Silence of the stars. How is it proved ?
> It isn't proved, you fool, it can't be proved.
> How can you prove a victory before
> It's won. How can you prove a man who leads,
> To be a leader, worth the following,
> Unless you follow to the death . . . . . .
> Well—God's my leader. And I hold that He is good
> Enough and strong enough to work His plan and purpose
> Out to its appointed end. [1]

Just one more thought before I close the chapter. In a letter which I received a little while ago the writer said this : ' Men and women need guidance. Poor souls are heart-broken, and struggling in the seas of sin and doubt, and they don't know where to go, whom to trust or what to believe. And they don't want to be mocked by negatives—they want realities.' I think that is true. That's why I said I think men are just as religious as ever—they are searching, groping—fumbling for Truth.

Well, I just want to conclude by saying this— Christianity does for men what nothing else can do. It does for man what man fails to do for himself. It takes the wreck from the road side, and with divine power lifts him up and bids him hope, and brings to his life something that transforms him. ' If a man be in Christ he is a new creature.' That's true. You may not be able to prove it logically. But you can't escape that—it's a demonstrated fact—something you can see for yourself. There are those in every church

[1] From ' Faith ' by Studdert Kennedy.

whose lives have been changed by the power of the Gospel of Christ. My own life has been changed. Now we are in the realm of fact. We can say I know. ' I know whom I have believed.' There are many, many things I cannot prove logically—but I believe in Christianity because it works. I've seen it, I've felt it—experienced it.

Now, what about you, my good reader ? You've probably puzzled and puzzled till you hardly know where you are. You've struggled in the dark till you are weary—just blindly groping, searching, struggling. And you do so much want to know, you want God. You'd like to believe in Him. Your heart is hot and restless without Him. And if you could believe in Him you feel that you would be able to believe more in yourself—your own possibilities and your own value.

Well, then, stop your struggling, striving and searching—just trust. ' Trust and obey, for there's no other way.' Have faith. A child doesn't struggle to know its mother—it just trusts her. You trust God. Throw yourself on Him, as it were, like Wesley when he sang, ' With faith I plunge me in this sea.' Take the risk—make the venture.

> With faith I plunge me in this sea,
> Here is my hope, my joy, my rest.

CHAPTER III

JESUS AND NATURE

Is God Cruel ?

WITH the coming of the spring there stole into my heart, a little while ago, an indescribable longing— a longing to break away from the common routine of everyday life, and to visit some sylvan scene where one could escape for a little while from the noise and rush of life, listen to the birds' songs, and refresh one's soul amid the stately architecture of some natural temple. It was a holiday time, and, as there were no meetings or pressing duties, I sought out a friend, and together we slipped away for a couple of days—

> Away, away from men and towns,
> To the wild woods and the downs,
> To the silent wilderness
> Where the soul need not repress
> Its longing.

The magic of the motor-car enabled us to leave home in the morning, and sleep in a little country town surrounded by the elfin witchery and fairy wonders of wild Wales. In a dream of delight we sped down the long roads, with the fresh green of the fields and hedges on either hand, through Worcester we passed, over the steepness of the Malvern hills, until the plains and fields spread out beneath us like a gorgeous carpet of exquisite design.

So we journeyed—through Ross and Monmouth to Tintern, where we lingered a long time enchanted by the loveliness of the Wye valley ; sauntering slowly and pensively through the woods, charmed by the pale loveliness of the primrose, the modest beauty of the celandine and the simplicity of the violet : taking delight in all the quiet life we saw. A sense of calm and repose pervaded everything. For a long time we lingered, watching the chaffinches and robins hop around us, and little by little there stole into our hearts something of a dreamful tranquillity.

Everything seemed unutterably peaceful, and we soon forgot all our busy schemes and aims, the tiny part we play in the world, with so much petty energy, such anxious responsibility. Even the flowers seemed to speak.

' Here,' they seemed to say, ' we bloom and brighten spring after spring. No one regards us, no one cares for us ; no one praises our beauty ; no one sorrows when these leaves grow pale, when we fall from our stems, when our dry stalks whisper together in the winter wind. But to you, because you have seen and loved us, we whisper our secret.' [1]

That night, as we sat over the fire in our hotel before turning in to rest, we indulged in a lazy desultory conversation—expressing random thoughts or lapsing into silence. And in one of the silences I began to wonder what I could preach about the following Sunday, and so expressed my thoughts aloud.

[1] Quoted from *The Thread of Gold*. Benson.

'Preach about Nature,' said my friend. 'I feel nearer to God in Nature than anywhere.'

That chance remark set me thinking. I, too, at times have felt very near to God's heart while wandering alone in wild woods. Once, while sauntering in a garden full of flowers I cannot name, I found, painted on the gate, the words

> One is nearer to God in a garden
> Than anywhere else on earth.

and I felt the words to be true.

There was a time in my youth when I was a sort of 'Nature worshipper'—I was a keen naturalist and argued with my anxious father that I did not feel a need to go to church because I could worship God better amid Nature's wildness. But since then I have beheld the beauty of the Christ, felt the irresistible charm of His personality and heard His challenges. And to one who has fallen in love with Jesus 'Nature worship' becomes a poor, even a pagan, practice.

I want in this chapter to tell you why. If Nature had been my only guide to God I should have been perhaps an agnostic or possibly an atheist.

*   *   *   *   *

For one thing, there is always in Nature a *sting*. Even the rose has its thorns. Beneath the beauty of purple heather there glides the sinister snake. Behind the light and shade of a wood there lurk foxes, stoats and weasels. And, hovering in the 'blue ethereal sky ' there are kestrels, eagles and hawks ready to swoop down upon their prey. And such things raise questions without answering them.

Supposing, for instance, you are sitting on a secluded slope about the hour of sunset. There is a soothing calm about everything—the sun dipping behind the hills, mists gathering in the hollows, and flowers at your feet. You feel, in such a place, a restfulness steal into your heart—it almost seems as though you can hear the still small voice of God. And then, in the grass below, you see a glint of brown fur. You sit perfectly still. A short distance away a carrion crow comes and perches on a straggling pine tree, like a black-coated sentinel. Then, in the grass immediately below, you catch sight of a stoat squatting on its hind legs with its forefeet resting on a stone, its beady eyes watching the grass in which you have seen the brown fur. The stoat's nose veers with the shifting breeze. Then, with amazing speed, it leaps across the grass and vanishes. A moment later the death-scream of a rabbit pierces the silence—and you turn to look at the crow, and realize that it is waiting to eat what the stoat leaves.

Such an incident awakens the scientist and philosopher in you—the scientist who sees, and the philosopher who questions. And the thoughts of God which have stolen into your heart, vanish as flowers vanish in winter. Questions begin to jostle their way through your mind—What sort of a God is it, who has made a world like this ? Nature may be beautiful on the surface, but beneath the smiling countenance there appears to be hidden the hideous grinning face of a fiend. Nature is ' red in tooth and claw.' The cuckoo shirks the responsibility of nesting. The hawk swoops down upon the sweet-songed bird in the bush. The owl hunts in the nocturnal shadows for shrews and mice, the fox cunningly steals the farmer's poultry. And, in other lands, fierce and repulsive beasts such as lions, leopards, crocodiles and cobras, lurk in the shadows, seeking something to devour.

And the thought of such blood-thirsty savagery brings a shudder to the mind. We often describe Nature in tender terms calling her ' Mother Nature,' or ' Dame Nature.' But she is not tender—she is savage and cruel. And thoughts such as these take the sweetness out of Nature. They turn the scent of flowers into the stink of carrion. . . . What sort of a God is there behind it all ? . . . Is there a God ? If so, is he cruel ? And so, through contact with Nature, we find ourselves up against baffling problems. We find ourselves in need of an elaborate philosophy to explain it all.

That was how it was in pre-Christian days. The primitive man looked about him at the wonders of the world in which he lived, and was impressed by the glory of sun and stars, awed by the majesty of mountains ; and terror-stricken by the ferocity of beasts, the terrors of storms and the fearfulness of earthquakes. He felt that it was all the work of some being or beings more cunning and powerful than himself, and began to people the forests with imaginary demons—spirits, part human, part beast, part fairy and part devil. He imagined he heard mystic voices in the night solitudes, and hung offerings on trees, or cast garlands into wells to please them. He invented these spirits in an effort to explain Nature.

But such childish fancies no longer satisfy man. Science has stripped Nature of her magic. Yet we are still conscious of the need of an explanation. We must have something to account for Nature : every effect has a cause. Some call that cause the ' Great Artificer,' some the ' Creative Force ' and others ' God.'

But even then, granting that Nature suggests to our minds the idea of a creator, the question is still unanswered as to what that creator is like. . . . Is he like his creation—a mixture of beauty and beastliness, of charm and cruelty ?

The Nature religions which still exist offer their explanations and theories—but they all leave one unsatisfied and uncertain. One thing only seems certain—that is, in Nature there is a unity and stability : Nature's laws are fixed and reliable ; and there appears to be running through it all a purpose —but a purpose we cannot guess !

But when we turn to Jesus Christ we do find something satisfying. It is true that Jesus does not solve all the questions with which the mind of man is confronted, but He offers a philosophy and a way of life which is far more satisfactory than anything else I know. It is a philosophy and principle which ends in good results—it works : its powers and value can be demonstrated : it results in humanitarianism, charity and brotherliness ! And, all through life, we judge the value of things not by their logicality, but by their efficacy.

I will not attempt to make a careful comparison between the paganism of the Nature lover and the humanitarianism of the Christ lover, but I will just suggest thoughts which may be helpful.

*   *   *   *   *

When sorrow comes your way, there is no comfort

in Nature. When you have been bereaved of your best-loved friend, when you feel stunned and dazed and broken-hearted ; you may find the silence and solitariness of Nature welcome—but they will not be comforting. They enable you to escape for a while from other people so that you may try to collect your thoughts : but after a while you will find that the solitariness and silence irritate you. In Nature's silence you may brood over your grief—but there will be no response, no sympathy, no compassion. The flowers will bloom just as beautifully as before—they will even thrive on the grave of your loved one ; but there are no tears shed in sympathy, no understanding hand-grip, no words of comfort. There is only a great beautiful smiling face with mystery reflected in its cold eyes.

Nature is unresponsive. Her indifference will mock you, her beauty intensify your grief, and her solitariness enhance your loneliness.

But when we turn to Jesus we find a sympathy which wept with bereaved friends, and hear from His lips words of comfort and consolation. We learn from Him that life is not so much an entertainment as an education, and that sorrow is one of her great teachers. After all, we never leave school, and we learn more from our sorrows than our joys. When we look at the Cross, we see that from the world's greatest anguish has come its greatest blessing. When we look into the face of Jesus and are told that God is like Him, we feel that such is a God worth worshipping. And when we turn to the story of the Resurrection we begin to feel a sense of hope, for there is a promise of immortality.

There is no hope in Nature. The only immortality she promises is that which comes with every spring— the promise that new life shall spring from rotting death. Nothing perishes in Nature—it only changes form. The flower that dies in the autumn does not die—it decomposes, and from its decomposed elements there springs another flower. And that is the only promise of immortality which Nature offers.

Here is a quotation from a modern Nature worshipper—a man of letters who does not share the orthodox belief in God, and claims that what makes the best in the human mind are ' the fields, the sparkle of running waters, the stars over the hill and the sunshine.'

' Last spring,' he writes, ' planting out sapling, beeches and fir trees with my little boy . . . I told him that one day he would have to build a big fire of faggots and dry branches, and burn me at night, when my ashes would float away on the wind, and sink into the ground, and rise again as grass in the rain and sunshine.'

That is all the hope of immortality his Nature religion offers. That was all he could teach his child about the meaning of death.

I am not going to launch out on a discussion as to the possibility of a personal immortality, and I must say in common honesty, that my views are too uncertain to permit dogmatism. But this I do believe —if there is no life beyond the grave, then this life with all its struggling and strife seems cruel and futile.

This life to my mind demands an immortality. But Nature offers no hope. And no belief in immortality often results in immorality. If there is nothing after death, then why worry ? Live as you jolly well like, do what you like, follow your animal instincts and appetites—go the pace. When you die you are done for : so, ' eat drink and be merry, for to-morrow we die.'

> Ah, make the most of what we yet may spend,
> Before we too into the dust descend ;
> Dust into Dust, and under Dust to lie,
> Sans Wine, Sans Song, Sans Singer, and Sans End !

Again, there is *no sense of sin in Nature*. Nature is non-moral ; it knows no right and no wrong—it lives by instinct—the instincts of production and preservation ; there is no idealism. Get what you can and never mind others ; fight for your life, and, if you are not strong enough or cunning enough to fight, you go to the wall, for in Nature only the fittest survive. Such a law may be all right for beasts, but it is not all right for men. Germany tried to apply that natural law to human life—and the whole world suffered. The theory that ' might is right ' and that ' the fittest survive ' drove the youth of Europe into soldiers' graves. ' By their fruits ye shall know them.'

Real Nature religion is devoid of ethics—it is a sentiment, but not a stimulus to morality. It sees and wonders, but does not lead to noble conduct and unselfish service. It admires the beauty of form and colour and sound which Nature provides, but it is indifferent to human needs. It is sensuous. It meditates but does not minister.

The Nature worshipper seeks solitude—he desires to be alone in the temple not made with hands. He is selfish. But one of the strongest of human instincts is the herd instinct—the longing for fellowship and communion. Man is a social being—he cannot live alone. His whole life is bound up with others—at every turn he is dependent on his fellows. And any religion which ignores the fact must inevitably break down. If man must have a religion, it must be a social and a sociable religion. The cry of the age is for ' team spirit '—individualism is all very well up to a point—but it is co-operation which is the need of the world.

And when we turn to Jesus we find One whose great stress was laid upon fellowship. His religion satisfies man's paramount need. There have been other teachers who have taught co-operation and socialism —but Jesus went one step further than any one else, and taught unselfishness and love. And He not only taught it, but lived it—He demonstrated its value and power. At the time of His death it seemed as though his theory and experiment had failed ; but as we look back now, we can see that He has succeeded in a unique way ! And at last, men are beginning to see that His is the only way !

Nature offers no redemption—if you have sinned you will find no forgiveness or promise of forgiveness in Nature. Her law is ' Sow tares and reap tares.' Your sin has been committed, and, because you are better than a beast, your conscience troubles you. But there is no cleansing, purifying power in Nature : her streams and springs may cleanse your body, but there is no cleansing for your soul. She is indifferent. You will never discover from Nature that God is Love, or that He forgives and offers redeeming strength. It needed Jesus to die upon a cross before we could realize that. I will not enter upon a detailed discussion of this point, and all I will say is—if I have to choose between a God who is like Nature and a God who is like Jesus—I choose the latter.

There are some men who create God in their own image; and there are others who try to re-create themselves in God's image. If you think of God as beastly, you will tend to be beastly. But if you think of God as love, you will tend to be loving. Your idea of God affects your morality, and your morality affects your value to society.

The Nature worshipper is something like a man mapping out the sea as land; marking waves as mountains. Nature has her dignity, poetry and appeal to the senses—but she lacks the power to inspire a high morality such as Christ presents—she appeals to the pagan within our hearts; Christ appeals to the divine. Nature worship is based on primitive awe and wonder, but Christianity is based on love and service—and there is a vast difference. The Nature worshipper looks at the world and feels that it must be the work of a power greater than himself, and the thought of a power greater than himself inspires awe, or even dread. And so worship comes through fear. But the religion of Jesus is not a religion of fear—it is a religion of trust. God is not to be thought of as great and dreadful—but as a Father who cares for His children. 'When ye pray, say " Our Father." '

*   *   *   *   *

The man who says he does not feel a need to come to church because he can worship God in Nature speaks unthinkingly or insincerely. Usually he is making a lame excuse ; sometimes he is a pagan—*i.e.*, one who is impressed by what appeals to ear and eye ; or, more often than not, he reads into Nature what he has learnt at his mother's knee or elsewhere of the Christ.

I said at the beginning, I was once a Nature worshipper myself. Let me add, that I still love Nature—but I love her because I read into her truths I have learnt from Christ. Looking at life purely as a scientist one gets baffled and bewildered ; but in Jesus and His way of life, one finds a guide who leads one into the Kingdom of Hearts Desire.

There are many questions I have not been able to answer for myself (and I suppose I never shall) but of this I am certain—to live Christ's way is the ONE WAY I know of putting into life all one can, and getting out of it all it can give. Jesus has brought new beauty and happiness to the world ; He has brought unspeakable joy to me ; He has robbed suffering of its sting ; and so I am content to leave many questions unanswered, and just try to follow Him.

Now, in comparing Nature worship with the religion of Jesus, I have been basing my arguments upon a great assumption—the assumption that Jesus was a historical person. The assumption is justified because most scholars are now agreed that the historicity of Jesus is beyond reasonable dispute.

But that is not enough. What was written in the Gospels about the life and death of Jesus might now be ancient history if the Gospels had told the whole story. But they did not, for the story is still being told. Thousands of men have lived and died, but the wonder of Jesus is that He died and still lives. You may marvel over His persistent power, but you cannot escape it ! After the Crucifixion something happened which made Christ's followers speak of His spirit as still alive. This belief was so strong that they spoke with the convictions of men who knew—they had seen and felt. And what they had seen and felt has changed the course of history.

Thus it is that a great scholar can write : 'Not all the other forces of history put together have done what Jesus has done for men. He is RISEN, and in the invincible power of His uprising is all our hope. The millions who have loved and believed in Him . . . have never thought of Him as dead, but as the Ever Living One whose life is the Light of the World.' [1]

In every human breast there are wistful longings, and I believe that they can only be satisfied in Jesus. No one can read His story without being conscious of the charm of His character, and without feeling that if every one lived like Him the world would be a different and more beautiful place.

I have already confessed that I never read the story of Jesus without feeling compelled to utter the prayer :

> I would be like Him,
> Show me the way.

And that's my religion—a religion of the love of Jesus. It is not a religion I have accepted in an emotional moment, or simply for sentimental reasons. I have embraced it after a long hard fight for faith, a long tussle with doubts, and a scientific study of Nature, history and psychology. After such study, and because of such study, I can honestly and sincerely

[1] *The Life of Christ.* R. J. Campbell, D.D. (Benn.)

say I believe that Christ's religion is the only religion which satisfies my intellect, my emotions and my whole being. It is a religion I can claim super-latively superior to the man who claims to find God in Nature, because it is a religion of comfort and hope—full of cheerful optimism ; it is essentially ethical—with its effects demonstrated in history and individual life ; it is a religion of usefulness because it is unselfish —it satisfies the herd instinct and is charged with a social significance ; and it is full of promise of a permanent peace for the world. And, finally, it is a religion of redemption—lifting above the world a Cross as its symbol—a symbol of salvation—salvation for the individual and salvation for society. To epitomize it all—it is a religion of Love ; claiming ' Thou shalt love the Lord thy God with all thy heart, and with all thy soul, and with all thy strength, and with all thy mind ; and thy neighbour as thyself.'

CHAPTER IV

JESUS AND INSTINCT

CAN WE CLIMB FROM THE GORILLA TO GOD ?

SOME few years ago many pious people were greatly concerned because Charles Darwin claimed that man shows signs of a relationship with the lower animals. It was suggested that men and monkeys were closely connected : and good, respectable people didn't like it ! (Men are usually ashamed of their poor relations.)

I am not in this chapter going to discuss the theory of evolution. All I will say is this : Speculate and theorize as you will, you must admit that there is in man something which can only be called bestial. Speaking for myself, I know that in my own ' make-up ' there's a bit of not only the monkey, but also the tiger : and I've to watch it lest it gets loose and does some damage !

I once saw a very pretty girl in a very ugly fit of temper, and I saw quite plainly in that pretty face the snarl of a tiger. In that moment of passion she jumped back into the jungle, and the expression on her face became exactly the same as the expression of an enraged animal facing its foe—the eyebrows knitted and arranged to protect the eyes from scratches, and the upper lip curled showing teeth and jaw set ready to bite ! She was beauty and beast rolled into one !

48

When people lose their tempers they become for the moment beasts. That's a fact few of us care to admit.

When you see a monkey in a zoo scratching itself and performing queer antics, you are amused ; but you hate to think that you could ever do anything to justify the idea that you have a blood relationship with such a low vulgar creature. But we all know plenty of people who can perform monkey tricks with such perfection that it is difficult to realize that they are not genuine jungle products.

Most of us do, in unguarded moments, display a remarkable resemblance to our jungle cousins. We preserve the family likeness. Of course, our civilization has done much to tame the brute in us—the claws have been clipped and the teeth extracted. But a brute is still a brute even though it be a tame brute ! And there is still enough brute about us to enable us to indulge in occasional brutality.

I do not hesitate in claiming that I consider myself a vast improvement on my distant ancestors who wore no clothes, hunted their food, and who banged their women on their heads with clubs before carrying them off in marriage ! We have progressed, I think, since those days. But I sometimes wonder just how far we have progressed. It is true we have our inventions—our telephones and gramophones, our telescopes and our talkies, our airplanes and our Amy Johnsons, our wireless waves and our marcel waves—and so on. But these things are not necessarily signs of progress.

When a man runs about naked, hunts his food, and lives in a forest, we call him a savage. But when

4

he wraps himself up in bandages called ' clothes,' and props himself up with crutches called ' furniture,' and amuses himself with toys called wireless sets, we say he is civilized. But his clothes and toys don't make him civilized any more than an admiral's uniform makes him an admiral. Refinement, culture and spiritual perception mean progress. And when I see so-called civilized men hurling tons of steel and lead at each other, dropping high explosives on towns in which are women and children, and digging for themselves trenches and dug-outs, in which to crawl and live like rabbits in warrens, caked with mud and covered with lice, I begin to wonder just how civilized they are.

As I look around the world of affairs, and turn over the pages of history, I see that there is only a very thin mask hiding the face of the beast.

I take up a newspaper (which is one of the symbols of civilization) and begin to read. I read of the affairs of State, of debates in the House of Commons, and so on. Then I read of a strike here, of a riot there, of a civil war somewhere, and of a rebellion somewhere else. I find whole pages devoted to murders, special pages for divorces, suicides and the like. And in these things I see, woven into the fibre of the paper as it were, the teeth of the tiger. You can't escape it. The beast may be silent, but he is never very far away.

We all have in us something akin to God ; but there is also something akin to a gorilla. In man's personality are possibilities of great good. But there are also possibilities of great evil. These are facts and we must face them scientifically. It's no use deluding ourselves that we are angels when we know

only too well that we are animals. We must, as
rational civilized creatures, seek to control the animal
nature and bring it into subjection to spiritual nature.

Most of us are ruled to a great extent, by our
animal instincts and tendencies. As one scientist
says, ' Man from the earliest days of babyhood acts
and re-acts according to the desire of his animal
instincts, far more than is commonly supposed.'

Most of us like to think we are guided chiefly by
our reason. But we are not. In ninety-nine cases
out of a hundred we are guided by instincts.

Let me illustrate. The boy who takes your gold
watch, opens it with his scout's knife, and stirs up
the works with a pin, is acting in response to his
instinctive tendency to be curious. The boy who
stands on the drawing-room sofa with a toy sword
in his hand, and, to the horror of his aunt, cries,
' I'm king of the castle—get down, you rascal ! ' is
acting in response to his instinct for self-assertion.

Perhaps some Sunday morning you make up your
mind to lie in bed instead of going to church. Then
someone cries ' Fire ! ' You are out of bed and in the
street in five seconds. You, urged by the emotion
of fear, respond to the instinct of self-preservation.
Then suppose someone tells you that your child is in
the burning house. The smoke and the flames will
not hold you back. It is the parental instinct which
has driven you back into the flames.

These simple illustrations are enough to show
that our animal instincts and tendencies control our
actions to a great extent. And it is no use being
ashamed of our instincts and pretending they don't
exist. If we do that, we shall be like a man sitting

on the safety valve of a steam engine. If you stop
up the safety valve the engine bursts. And instincts
are like that. It doesn't do to fasten them up. They
are like a river—if you don't want it to flow through
your fields you can either dam it or cut another
channel and redirect it. If you dam it there will be
a flood.

We must redirect our instincts as we would redirect
a river. For instance, take the instinct of curiosity
which makes the boy poke your watch with a pin.
The instinctive tendency of curiosity is quite natural.
When directed one way it can lead a person into being
a busy-body, and a scandal-monger and a nuisance to
society. But when directed another way it leads one
into paths of scientific research and makes one a
benefactor to society. The same instinct makes the
scandal-monger, the detective and the scientist. It all
depends upon the channel into which the instinct is
directed. The same instinct directed in one way
becomes a curse, and in another a blessing.

Often boys who have been the worst at school
have turned out the best men. This is because the
animal anger and passion which in childhood are
manifested in the stamping of feet or the flying into
a paddy, can, if rightly directed, become a passion
for truth and a hatred of evil.

Naturally I'm a fighter. I used to fight when
a boy, and even now have pugnacious if not pugilistic
propensities ! But I have tried to direct that instinct
into a good channel and fight for the truth.

We all have these animal tendencies and instincts,
and we must see that they are properly directed.
Perhaps you have a tendency to hate. Well then,

direct that tendency so that you hate not men but evil. Perhaps you are passionate—well then, be passionate in the cause of truth and right.

One of the most powerful animal instincts we have to deal with is the herd instinct. Just as buffaloes, wolves or baboons live together in herds, so do men. Most men would rather live with people they hate and detest than live alone. They would rather live together and quarrel every day than live alone. When rightly directed this instinct leads to fellowship, social good, co-operation : when wrongly directed it leads to quarrels, feuds and wars.

Wars are mass returns to the jungle in which armies and navies take the place of teeth and claws. And we pretend that all this fighting business is something very glorious. We talk of patriotism and the rest of it ; we sing of the Land of Hope and Glory, and tell our children how their grandfathers and great-grandfathers fought nobly and died bravely in this cause or that.

It is quite true that some of those grandfathers may have fought because they thought they were doing a noble thing. But it's time we began telling our children that fighting is a thing for beasts and not men. Our job is not to gloat over the memory of the fights our grandfathers arranged, but to set to work to redirect the fighting instinct into fresh channels. If there is any fighting to be done it must be against the beasts in our own hearts.

And that is exactly what Jesus taught, although He taught it by implication more than by definite statement. He suggested that the law of ' an eye for an eye and a tooth for a tooth ' (which is the law of the jungle) should be replaced by the law of 'love one another' (which is the law of the Kingdom of Heaven). He even went so far as to suggest that anger is a crime in God's eyes. It appears that in His day one could be brought before a court of law for calling any one 'raca' just as to-day one can be fined for using bad language. And Jesus suggested that to insult or despise another is to bring on oneself not only the judgement of a court but also of God.

In the Sermon on the Mount, Jesus told His hearers that they could not find God without first making an honest attempt to come to terms with any brother with whom, for one reason or another, they had lost contact. I don't think we have yet realized the tremendous significance of this! I believe that one reason why so many Churches are weak spiritually, and not doing the work they ought to, is that the members are harbouring grievances.

I was told, only a short while ago, of a conversation between two friends who had not met for some time. One asked the other how things were going in the church. 'I've stopped going,' said Mrs. X.

'How's that?' asked Mrs. Y.

Mrs. X said: 'There was so much friction; so many quarrels and backbitings among the members that I got heartily sick of it all, and now my husband and I go for motor-rides on Sundays instead.'

Now that's not a fairy tale: it's a fact, and a very unpleasant fact, too. But we must not shirk it because it is unpleasant. If there's a dead rat under your pantry floor, it's no use holding your nose and pretending it's not there: you must pull up the boards and remove the source of offence. Some of our characters are like pantries with dead rats rotting beneath the boards. Jealousies, backbitings, and bitterness are all too common in Christian congregations. So many want to be big frogs in little pools, and so many have perverted curiosity complexes, that true fellowship becomes impossible. And then we wonder why our churches are badly attended.

Jesus makes it perfectly clear that before we can get right with God we must be willing to leave no stone unturned to get right with men. In other words, we are to strive to be angels and not animals. We are to live in fellowship as brothers, and not fight as beasts. We are to direct our low tendencies into high channels.

One sometimes hears a person say, ' No one can come between me and my God.' Of course everything depends upon the nature of your God. Many people worship the God of Self—and of course no one can get between Self and Self. But if your God is the God of Jesus, then others can come between you and your God. From a Christian standpoint you can't have true worship without true fellowship.

Have you ever tried to pray and found that your cherished bitterness against some unfriendly person made real praying impossible ?

You remember when Macbeth tried to pray after his murder of Duncan the prayer ' stuck in his throat.'

Think of someone you dislike. Then kneel down and pray for him. And pray so sincerely that, if the very next moment you have a chance of helping that person, you will do it. That's what Jesus suggests we are to do always. We are to live in a spirit of forgiveness which results in fellowship.

This was all strange to the people of His day. The pagan world thought it was 'infra dig' to forgive—it was a sign of weakness. But Jesus insisted all through His life that the spirit of forgiveness is the essence of discipleship, and the stuff of which the Kingdom is to be made, because the Kingdom is a fellowship, and you can't have a fellowship without forgiveness. 'When you pray say forgive us . . . as we forgive others, for if ye do not forgive men God will not forgive you !' What a staggering statement!

Peter once said, 'How often shall my brother sin against me, and I forgive him ? '

And Jesus said, 'Seventy times seven !'

And Jesus didn't only preach the doctrine, He practised it—even on the cross ! 'Father forgive them, for they know not what they do,' He said. Over and over again He kept on saying it, as the cross was raised from the ground and dropped into its socket so that He was thrown forward on the nails as they tore His hands and feet. He kept on saying it, steadily and persistently—'Forgive them.'

The Church is Christ's body, and if it is His body it must be vitalized by His blood. And His blood is the blood of forgiveness which was shed on Calvary for the sins of men. We are to be a body of people who have been loved into being lovers, who have been forgiven so much ourselves that we can forgive others over and over again. We are to be a fellowship of His followers, and you *must* forgive to preserve a fellowship.

But the Church has not carried out this ideal—the ideal of forgiveness has always been too big for the Church—there has always been too much of the beast just beneath the surface. And so, over and over again Christ has been unable to find a place in the Church which bears His name, and has had to leave the lily-scented altars, and the stately buildings and make His appeal outside. And there, in street and market-place, He has gone on with His work while the Church has gone on with its quarrels. But, wherever He has gone, there have always been a few faithful and large-hearted followers who have gone with Him.

I would like to suggest, as my closing remark, that you and I be brave enough to go with Him. That we be large hearted enough to forget the insults and wrongs, and follow the example of the One who, hanging from a cross, prayed, ' Forgive them.' In other words, to be disciples of the Nazarene we must be apostles of Love—' God is love,' and you cannot worship Love except in the spirit of Love. Only in the Temple of Love do we really worship. It is not so much by buildings, by hymns and prayers that we really worship, as by kindly words, sympathetic attention and love. The real places of worship are by the bedsides of sufferers, in the arms of little children, in centres of social services—in a love which is big enough to forgive, and powerful enough to go where others would not go.

I began with the beast ; I end with benevolence ; for, it seems to me, we climb from the brutal to the beautiful by that ladder—the ladder of love.

Thou shalt love . . .

CHAPTER V

JESUS AND PEACE

Is Peace Contrary to Nature?

DURING my boyhood days our most popular game was ' soldiers '—we were never so happy as when, with helmets on our heads and toy swords and drums fastened to our belts, we paraded the back garden with all the pomp and dignity of Life Guards.

All boys are more or less bloodthirsty, and like other lads our immature minds were full of battles and sieges, bombardments and skirmishes, and such vain imaginings. Then, one day, my Dad (whom I thought infallible) told me there was going to be a mighty big war—a war which, he thought, would last a mighty long time, and, he added, ' I hope, Laddie, you'll never have to go.' It seemed ridiculous that he should fear that I—a child—should have to join the ranks of the khaki-clad and fight for King and Country.

Then came August of 1914 with the declaration of war—the streets began to fill with soldiers, men drilled in the open spaces, the sight of guns and prancing horses thrilled us, and we spent our pennies on vivid war pictorials, and acted the scenes we saw there portrayed. Then the excitement passed and we tired of the whole business. Boylike we did not realize its true significance.

58

But when one morning, just as we were having breakfast, enemy gun boats opened fire on our town, and we saw houses all around us being blown to pieces, and some of our neighbours killed—among them a little baby—then we began to realize what it all meant, and the horror of the things began to impress us.

Then came the spring again, with warm sun and meadows gay with flowers. War had no effect on minnows and tadpoles and missel thrushes—and bird nesting and outdoor activities mercifully helped us to forget. But the summer passed and still the war continued. Food became scarce. Zeppelins proved a menace to our town by night, and submarines by day. Men whom we knew marched away with a splendid swing singing ' Tipperary ' and never returned. The women seemed to be eternally knitting and sending off parcels to the Front. Then the senior boys of the school put on khaki and marched away like the rest —many of them never to return.

And so the ghastly business went on for four years, and then came the Armistice followed by treaties, conferences, pacts, and the activities of the League of Nations. And now we are all talking ' Peace.'

But do we want Peace ? There are those who tell us that Peace means stagnation—that it is War which brings the best out of us. Strife is the law of life, we are told. You see it everywhere. When we boys played at soldiers we were satisfying a craving or an instinct—an innate craving for strife. You see this craving both in Biology and History.

The biologist tells us that everywhere in Nature is strife. Nature is ' red in tooth and claw.' The whole of the carnivorous creation KILLS in order to live.

And, adds the cynic, man kills for the pleasure of killing. You cannot get away from it—we are always killing. And it is mere sluggishness of imagination which makes us sometimes forget the fact, because the killing, in civilized cities at any rate, is hidden away like other messy things and performed by special classes of people. We kill sheep and oxen, fishes and fowls for food, we hunt and kill foxes and otters for sport, we kill seals for their skins, and whales for their oil—we are always killing. Our hands are red with blood. And this constant killing is one of the fundamental and primary facts of life.

Let me illustrate.

About the beginning of this century it was decided by the Turkish government that the pariah dogs which filled the streets of Constantinople must be removed. To kill them would have been repugnant to Turkish feelings : so the dogs were collected in some thousands and deported to an uninhabited island. There was nothing much to eat ; only a few rats, rabbits, and the like. The hungry dogs first ate the other animals and then one another. They starved and fought and died, until after a time the howling ceased.

That illustrates the undeniable, biological fact that life is maintained by eating other animals or else by eating their food. Thus we see that life is not based on peace : it is based on an unrelenting murderous struggle.

Turning from biology to history we see the same thing. From the beginning of human history there have been wars—tribal conflicts, national struggles, and finally the World War. In a single century England alone has fought eighty wars. War seems to be a law of life.

But there is an element we have forgotten. Let us return again to the story of the pariah dogs. Some of those dogs had puppies, and the male dogs tried to eat them—it was an easy way of getting food. But the mother dogs fought like tigers to defend their young—fought against odds and died. There you see a new element entering into life—something which is very much like love—something which will, at any rate, sacrifice and die to save its object.

And still sticking to the realm of biology one can pursue the subject still further and discover that the law of kill-to-live becomes increasingly suffused and penetrated by the law of co-operate-to-live. In the animal world a whole herd or flock will act as one in the interests of all. And that often involves an actual sacrifice of self by the individual for the sake of the whole.

Thus, if it is a law that animals cannot live without killing, it is also a law that they cannot live without, in some sense, co-operating and sacrificing themselves for others. And the higher you get in the scale of creation the truer that becomes.

The biologist claims that man is a highly developed animal and that the laws which apply to the lower creation apply also to him. We can see how true that is by a glance at history. We'll take Old Testament history as an example. In the Old Testament you find individuals like Cain living for themselves and fighting their individual battles. Then you find the members of families (like that of Abraham) working together, and living—not so much for the sake of the individual —but for the group of individuals which forms the family—and the family fights to protect and support itself. Then families joined together in tribes and each family worked and fought for the good of the tribe. Then the tribes co-operated and formed nations—and each tribe worked and fought for the good and protection of the nation.

Nature and History then, compel us to admit that life *is* based on strife *and* co-operation. Co-operative strife, if you like. You have it everywhere—in the jungle, in savage tribes, and even in our own civilization. In commerce you have firms co-operating in the struggle to make things better and sell them cheaper than others. In education you have men co-operating to equip themselves mentally better than others. In religion you have men co-operating in their struggle against temptation. Co-operative strife is everywhere.

Well then, what about all this Peace talk ? Do we really want peace ? Would peace be good for us ? Would it not be contrary to nature ? Would not peace mean that we should languish and become soft and flabby and eventually fizzle out ? If by Peace you mean repose, or an absence of effort and striving, we certainly do not want it.

But, *you can have strife without war.* It is obvious that if man is to remain virile and robust he must not shirk strife. Thus, a peace to be permanent and beneficial must be a peace based on strife. (That I know, sounds like a paradox—but it is nevertheless true.) There are native tribes in Africa who live a life of ease. They are fed by what they call the bread tree, and are clothed by the simple vegetation around them. How simple such a life seems, and in certain moods how attractive. But we do not go to Central

Africa for the great leaders of the world. We go to the lands of grey skies and bitter winds and challenging climates for the men who shape humanity's destiny. The very fact that we, in Great Britain, have had to struggle and combat has developed in us the spirit of endurance and triumph. Struggle and strife have made us what we are.

Peace does not mean the subduing of effort. It means rather the controlling and directing of effort. When a boy plays at soldiers it is not really the bloodshed which appeals to him—it is the effort, the struggle.

If you show a crowd of boys and girls two pictures illustrating different ways of settling disputes—the one, a cavalry charge, with horses straining at the bit and soldiers yelling and fighting ; the other a group of bald-headed cabinet ministers sitting round a table—almost every child will secretly be in favour of the cavalry charge. But it is not that they want to kill (most of them would be scared at the sight of a corpse) but they want to face peril. They want adventure—they want to put forth for one moment the extreme effort of mind and body of which they are capable.

I think it is obvious that life without strife means decay. Sit in an easy chair all day and you lose the use of your muscles and become soft and flabby and good for nothing. Pet and pamper a child and keep it out of harm's way, and then when it is left to itself and a crisis comes it is unable to grapple with difficulty and goes under. To remain vigorous and strong physically, mentally and morally you must struggle and strive.

In seeking to establish a peace then, we must have a peace which satisfies the strife craving. We must not cut out strife, but direct it into useful channels. We must strive not for the conquest of other nations so much as for the conquest of ourselves —and not from selfish or personal motives, but from social motives. We must strive after personal perfection in order to attain social perfection. We must replace our national aims by world aims. We must replace patriotism by altruism. We are all part of the great machine we call civilization, and (quite apart from any religious ideas) it is our duty to work and strive for the improvement, preservation and protection of that civilization. Self-improvement for the sake of society is our duty.

The peace, then, which will bring sanity and stability back to the world must be no gentle, persuasive thing, no dove with olive branches and brooding eyes, but a more magnificent warrior than war itself. War HAS its majesty and grandeur and even creative power—and we must remember that— and in establishing a new peace we must seek to make it more majestic and attractive and creative than war.

Lovers of peace have done their cause harm by representing it as a soft security, and not as the living, working, fecund splendour that it is. Peace is not negative but positive. Not cessation from activity, but worth while activity. It is not like a Hindu sitting in the sun asleep, but rather like a gardener busy attending his plants and reaping the harvest. Peace—the kind of peace the world needs—is a thing of broad acres, of gardens and granaries full. It involves the opening of continents. It stands for enterprise, experiment, adventure, advancement. For books and music and all the sweet foolish intimacies that bring bliss into our lives. We shall never end war with a belief in the old placid peace. We shall never end it by a mere war hatred. We must first recognize war's power to stir the spirit, and then, strong in our knowledge, make peace a stirring passion, too.

*   *   *   *   *

We have seen how in the past man struggled and fought first for his own glory and protection, then for the glory of the family, and later the glory of the nation. The latter was the attitude of the last generation. We talked of our national pride, we sang ' Land of Hope and Glory,' we prated about King and Country and preached patriotism.

Now all that is all right and has done its work, just the same as strikes have done their work. But strikes as weapons are obsolete ; and so is patriotism and the wars which were its weapons. We have grown out of patriotism—or we ought to have done. We have gradually reached a point in our development when national protection must be replaced by world protection. In the future it must not be ' King and Country,' but ' God and Civilization.' Otherwise we shall commit racial suicide.

We are told that man will always fight for self-protection. True. But war no longer means self-protection but self-extermination. War has become such a diabolically cunning, scientifically cruel, and economically chaotic affair that civilization can no longer bear it. The strain is too great. A limited strain will strengthen the muscles, but a strain too hard and too long tears them. And the strain of a war like the Great War has a three-fold effect—it

5

destroys manhood, it makes men brutes, and shatters civilization.

The Great War destroyed ten million men—among them artists, musicians, politicians, poets and the like —they were debarred by the war from giving their best gifts to the world—Europe became for a time a continent to which such gifts were no use. It did not require expert construction, but expert destruction.

The war made men brutes. In a civilization the brute instincts and passions are controlled. In war they are encouraged. For instance, if someone makes you angry you have an impulse to knock him down. But you control the impulse. Otherwise the world would be a bear garden. But in war the tables are turned and anger and hatred and lust are encouraged. You return to the jungle. You shatter that which it has taken millions of years to create. War is incompatible with civilization. It interrupts and makes impossible the main task of mankind—the two-fold task of raising individual character and the formation of a better society.

War repudiates social laws. Things which are criminal in peace become legitimate in war. We open our prisons and release those who are normally a menace to our civilization, give them arms and tell them to do their worst. Every weapon, every method, every form of violence, fraud and cunning is considered legitimate for the sake of victory. When a nation is at war her subjects spell reason with a T. That leads to the continuation of such conduct after the war is over.

Again, men who are facing death for the sake of country are shown great indulgence, and licence is forgiven and even smiled at. Then the licence spreads to those who are not facing death. If Tom who fights is allowed to go the pace why not John who does not fight ?

Wars are won not by reason, scrupulousness, and fairness, but by the opposites—push, violence, ruthlessness, trickery and treachery. And a generation brought up in such an atmosphere cannot be expected to live according to the fair and lawful methods which are essential for a good society. Education and discipline, of course, suffer, too. War then, means loss of standard. War does not mean self-preservation but waste—

> Waste of muscle, waste of brain,
> Waste of patience, waste of pain,
> Waste of manhood, waste of health,
> Waste of beauty, waste of wealth,
> Waste of blood, waste of tears,
> Waste of youth's most precious years,
> Waste of ways the saints have trod,
> Waste of glory, waste of God.
> (STUDDERT KENNEDY.)

If civilization is to be safeguarded, if society is to be saved from self-suicide it must be by co-operation. Nurse Cavell as she faced death said, 'Patriotism is not enough.' It is not enough. Be proud of your nation if you can—but remember your nation is only a section of civilization—we are all human beings together and we must work in the spirit of unity and not of enmity. If individuals can work for the family, and families for tribes, and tribes for nations, then nations must now work for civilization.

* * * * *

Now, I have tried carefully and logically to reach

a conclusion. But Jesus came to the same conclusion 1,900 years ago and put it in a far simpler way when He taught brotherhood and service. Jesus, then, makes not only a religious contribution, but states a truth and a principle which is imperative for the continuation of civilization. It is only in His teaching that civilization can be saved. And the Church must lead the way. We are beginning to practise brotherhood in small ways, but we shirk practising it in a big way. We have brotherhoods of Freemasons, brotherhoods of Scouts and so on—why not a brotherhood of nations.

That is what we must strive for. In war we take tremendous risks—we must be prepared to take risks in peace. We have been brave enough to fight; now we must be brave enough to disarm.

It is imperative that all peoples of the world should not look backward, but forward, and that we should leave behind our prejudice and fear and hatred and malice as part of the savagery we wish to rise above, and that we should seek—nay, strive—to cultivate a spirit of co-operation and establish a united civilization, just as we have a United States or a United Kingdom.

In his novel, *The Enemy*, Channing Pollock describes with wonderful vividness, the effects of war upon a middle-class family. It is a story of love and marriage; with its joys, its ambitions and its tragic moments, such as was being played all over Europe in every walk of life during those terrible days.

Pauli, a professor's daughter, is married to an author. Just as his play is to be produced, war breaks out and he has to go. Then follow those terrible four years —years of anguish, suspense and privation. The professor is turned out of the university owing to his pacifist views. He has to sell his furniture to obtain money. Food is scarce and dear. Pauli's child dies for want of nourishment. And while some starve, others, who have kept back food supplies till prices are high, grow rich.

Then, the day Pauli's husband is expected on leave news comes of his death. Other men return maimed and broken—a musician minus his fingers and wrecked with shell shock shoots himself. An editor returns a physical and mental wreck and cannot find work. So the story unfolds itself—not exaggerated, but all the incidents bearing the unmistakable stamp of truth.

At the end of the story a little group of friends are standing about in the professor's drawing-room talking. Outside in the street children can be heard playing at soldiers. The friends are discussing the war, and one, looking through the window at the playing children is saying, ' World wide chaos and— the next generation—drilling ! '

' Yes,' says Pauli, ' the next generation and perhaps the next. But oh ! time isn't measured by our little lives. All this can't be for nothing. There's a new spirit in the world, a new rebellion. Ten million dead, for every man a wife or mother crying, " No more war ! " Millions more who saw and suffered, crying, " No more War ! " And from those millions, millions yet to come, always wiser and kinder, until the whole world sees and understands and cries, " No more hate ! No more prejudice ! No more War ! " '

From the courtyard, from across the hall, comes the sombre roll of drums. The professor, entering quietly, closes the door and his eyes very grave he says :

'God give us tolerance!'

'God give us love,' adds another.

'God give us peace,' says a third.

Such should be the prayers of all who profess to follow the Christ—God give us tolerance! God give us love! God give us Peace!

CHAPTER VI

JESUS AND IDEALISM

Does Experience Shatter One's Belief in Idealism?

WHEN I was in my teens a successful business man addressed me something like this : ' Ah, yes, when one is young one is naturally idealistic—youth always builds its castles in the air ; but as you grow older you will learn to be practical—you will find that your ideals break up like clouds. Age brings one down to earth with a bump—it forces one to a belief in practical politics.'

I am some twelve years older now than I was when that was said, and what has really happened is just the opposite of what was prophesied would happen ! I have not lost my ideals—I have increased my belief in them ! If I have lost anything it is my faith in successful business men who talk glibly about practical politics. Experience has taught me that ideals are more powerful than practical politics, that their influence is wider and more abiding.

Walk with me through the Museum of History—what do we see ? Some four hundred years before Christ, we see Athens staking its all on an elaborate democracy—the Athenian constitution of that time, we are told, became the most completely democratic that the world has yet seen.   Practical politics !   At the same time we see her poisoning her idealist—Socrates.   But Socrates still has his influence while the Athenian democracy is forgotten ; or, if remembered, remembered as a failure.   Then we see the Roman Empire stretching out its hands north and south, east and west in an effort to possess the Earth. Practical politics !   And, as with Athens so with Rome, we see her destroying the age's idealist—Jesus Christ.   But Rome decayed—her politics failed.   But the ideals of Christ spread, gathered force and still dominate the thoughts and lives of men !   Then, in recent years, we see men like Keir Hardie staking their all on political systems.   But as they near the end of Life's journey we find their buoyant optimism replaced by a significant hesitancy—' I often feel very sick at heart with politics ! ' Hardie is reported to have said, ' If I were a thirty years younger man . . . I would methinks . . . go forth among the people to proclaim afresh and anew the full message of the Gospel of Jesus of Nazareth.'   The same business man who laughed at my ideals is now caught in the grip of his own machinery —he is literally a slave to his business : longing to be free he is unable to release himself from the prison he has built up around himself.   He now tells me that he has learnt by painful experience that money is not everything and that he is convinced that it is religion which really matters.

The world is full of these so-called practical people. They will tell you that they are the sort of people who always take things as they are ; they tolerate no idealistic nonsense.   They don't act on theories—they believe in facing facts !   But when we look round to

see what successes they have made, what do we find ?
No doubt their business is a ' going concern,' and no
doubt there is a big balance at the bank. But
frequently there is a wretched state of affairs at home
—they have no time for home life, and so wife and
children go their own way. Their business worries
so weigh upon them that they become hard in disposition and often bad tempered at home. In the
industries and states which they try to control we
find suspicion and discontent. And in a wider sphere,
a world suffering from shell shock. Looking back only
a few years we find that their practical politics have
resulted in pugnacious practices and culminated in a
War which has done its worst to wreck the world.

When idealists venture to suggest that the meek
shall inherit the earth and that you can conquer more
effectively by returning good for evil, than evil for
evil, these practical people bellow ' Absurd ! '
' Nonsense ! '

But history shows that ideals succeed where practical
politics fail. Idealists have abolished homicide, infant
labour, gladiatorial games, punishment by torture,
monarchic tyranny and human slavery. And they
shall abolish war !

The practical man says that things cannot be done
with conditions as they are. Which is true. But the
idealist changes the conditions. The practical person
achieves the possible, the idealist the impossible.
The practical man keeps his nose to the grindstone and
so sees only sand, steel and sparks. The idealist lifts
his eyes to heaven and so sees suns and stars. The one
sticks to his grindstone and so sharpens his sword—
but he perishes by the sword. The other looks to

heaven and may be rewarded only by a cross—but that cross converts the world. The practical man says ' My neighbour is armed and so I shall arm '—but when two men are armed a fight invariably follows. The idealist says ' swords mean suspicion and suspicion means strife ; but trust means peace and peace means prosperity.'

We have a tendency to use catchwords and phrases —and we run them to death. We get a pet word and use it on every occasion as though it had a magic power. A sort of ' open sesame.' ' Evolution ' is such a word. ' Revolution ' is another. ' Reform ' another. Personally of the three I prefer ' reform ' for ' reform ' implies form. It suggests that we are trying to shape something in a particular image— that we want a world of a particular type, or a life of a particular nature. That we are trying to make the world and human life like something we already see in our minds. Everything depends upon that something we see—in other words upon our ideals. ' Reform ' suggests that we see something out of shape that we mean to put into shape—and we know what shape. ' Evolution ' is just unfolding. Revolution is just turning things the other way up. Reform is re-shaping. Reform and idealism go hand in hand. Idealism the dynamic, reform the resulting process.

The trouble with many people is that they never know quite what they do want to make of life or the world. They are always changing the model. And the result is that they never make anything, except a mess. Let us suppose an artist one day sets himself the task of painting a Madonna. The following day his mood changes and he decides to make her into an

angel. Then another day he decides a fairy would be
more to his fancy. Another day he decides he ought
to have made her into a nun. Then another day, a
nurse. What sort of a picture would it be? It
would rival any impressionist or futurist caricature.
A Madonna's eyes, an angel's dress, a fairy's wand, a
nurse's cuffs and a nun's rosary and cross. A mad
medley of miscellaneous models.

But, you say, no artist outside an asylum would be
mad enough to do that. And yet that is how thousands
of people (all outside asylums) try to shape their lives.
Their ideals and principles change like the wind.
One day they want to be saints and another to turn
the world into a palace of pleasure. One day their
ambition is to be rich, another to found a democracy.
They are ascetics one day, and hedonists the next.
They read a society novel and see a society film and
their great desire is to be aristocrats, and they become
fastidious about their dress and precise in their
manners. But the next week they read of a Tolstoy
renouncing his wealth and position, and their great
desire is to be humble and a friend to the poor. Their
lives jerk up and down like lines on the temperature
chart of a fever patient. Their vision is always changing, with the result that their lives are always pretty
much the same—they want to be everything and end
by being nothing. They aim at this, that and the other
—and miss the lot. No ideals hold them long enough
to be realized. You don't change your status as
long as you keep changing your mind. To be of
use your ideal must be fixed. If every time an artist
looked up from his canvas he found a fresh model
posing, his picture would never be finished. Ideals

are models, we are the artists, life is the canvas. The model must be fixed if the picture is to be painted, and the ideal must be fixed if the life is to be perfected.

We talk a lot to-day about Socialism. The word sounds well; it sounds as though it means much and can do a lot. But perhaps it does not mean and do all it sounds it will. The Socialist says we must have better conditions and decent houses. Quite! But better conditions and decent houses will not solve all our problems. There are those who talk as though decent houses would abolish wretchedness. But take a walk around a council house estate. The houses are decent, and many of them respectable. But there are also many which are wretched. Reform depends not so much upon changed conditions as on changed vision. Change a man's environment and leave his vision the same, and soon his environment conforms to the nature of his vision. But change his vision and his environment changes accordingly. Put a drunkard out of a slum into a decent house. Soon his house becomes a slum. But convert a drunkard in a slum and his house becomes a home—respectable and clean. His vision changes his environment. The weakness of Socialism is that it emphasizes the need of changed conditions and forgets the need of changed conduct.

A modern novelist tells the story of an athlete who had a great passion for beauty. One day he brought home a beautiful vase, and placed it in his sitting room. But the beauty of the vase made everything else seem drab and ugly. So slowly he had to change all the furniture to harmonize with the beautiful vase. In other words his vision changed his environment. I have known drunkards clad in rags, their homes devoid of furniture, who, on their conversion to Christianity have become respectable, well dressed, and made their homes clean and cosy. Their changed vision changed their environment.

We hear much talk about equality of opportunity, as though reducing everything to a dull level would make for universal happiness. But a dull level means monotony, and monotony means unhappiness. History and biography have shown that those with the least opportunities have often turned out the most successful ; while those with many opportunities often have so many to choose from that they end by choosing none at all. The solution is not in environment but in man. And that is where Christianity differs from Socialism. Christianity is socialistic in that it dreams of a better and cleaner world. But it differs from Socialism in that its methods of bringing about that better world are very different. Socialism, in effect, says change conditions and man will improve. Christianity says change man and conditions will improve. There is the difference.

Jesus did not set out with a political programme endeavouring to reorganize a state, remodel towns or reconstruct houses. He simply set out to change men's minds. He chose twelve men and revolutionized their outlook—changed their scales of values. And in that way He began to change the world. Through the changed vision of those twelve men there eventually came the elevation of womanhood, the smashing of racial barriers, the abolition of slaves, and the spread of that humanitarianism which has resulted in hospitals, poorhouses, and all manner of philanthropic institutions. There were Socialists long before Christ, but we seldom hear of what those Socialists did. But you cannot escape what Christ has done. His influence is manifest everywhere. 'By their fruits ye shall know them.'

I am not saying that politics are no use—only that they need ideals to act as a dynamic.

Of course, one must be practical, but one should be ideally practical. One must, for instance, be practical in running a house. If you only earn £3 a week, it is the height of folly to spend £3 10s. But you can be practical without being prosy. Be poetically practical. If you are running a home make it an ideal home— the best you can conceive. Even though you do only get £3 a week, you can still have love and beauty and truth. Your walls may want papering and your furniture may be moth-eaten, and your pictures ugly. And if that is your only idea of a home they will always remain so. But if you have in your mind an ideal home your home will inevitably begin to shape itself to your ideal. It may take years but it will come.

So with a State. There may be much in the State you consider ugly and wrong. If you just accept it as the inevitable it will remain so. But as long as there is a vision of a better world, a better world will be in the making.

So too (which is far more important) with life. If you are content with your life as it is, it will remain as it is. But if you dream of a life which is better than yours—more beautiful, more useful; purer and nobler; then inevitably your life will begin to shape itself according to your ideal. Someone has said ' as we think, so we become.' If your ideal man is a Nero—cruel, cynical, greedy, gluttonous, lazy and licentious—then you tend to become a Nero. If, on the other hand, your ideal is a Christ—compassionate, great-hearted, gentle, loving, and kind—then you tend to become like Him. Ideals do not let us down with a bump—they elevate us. Ideals are everything. What our ideals are that we tend to become.

What is your ideal of life ? Have you ever thought about it ? Have you ever asked yourself ' What is my life ? ' What does it mean ? What ought I to make of it ? Is there a purpose in life ? ' Every effect has a cause ' says science. ' Every life has a purpose ' says religion. It is difficult to dogmatize as to what the purpose of life is—perhaps it is perfection. ' Be ye perfect as your Father in heaven is perfect.' And there we are brought again face to face with Christ. When we talk of human perfection we think of Him. He is the ideal. Every one has to admit His supremacy. He is the model. From Him the picture should be painted. G. K. Chesterton writes, ' God has given us not so much the colours of a picture as the colours of a palette. But He has also given us a subject, a model, a fixed vision. We must be clear about what we want to paint.'

No one, I think, having beheld the beauty of Christ could wish for anything better. Jesus is the ideal. We have seen that when we cast aside our prejudices and our preconceived ideas we feel an impulse just to kneel before Him and say ' I would be like Him, show me the way.' And when we do that, life is already being perfected. With that prayer the ideal becomes a dynamic and reacts on conduct. And that is the secret of Christianity's success. As Paul says, ' The love of Christ constraineth us.'

A story is told by Professor Drummond, which shows the wonderful effect the love of Christ has on the outward manner of a person in whose soul it is found. A Scottish lassie had been quite transformed from her former self by some secret power within, and had become the most lovable of characters. Some time afterwards the girl was stricken with a fatal disease, and on her dying bed was asked what had wrought the change in her life. Taking from her breast a tiny locket she said : ' Inside here you will find the secret of all I have done for Christ. Do not open it till I am gone where I shall know sorrow no more.' When the spirit passed away the locket was opened, and on a slip of paper were found written the words ' Whom, having not seen, we love.' There was the secret of the girl's life—Jesus was her ideal. But He was something more than an ideal—He was an inspiration. Just to copy a good example does not do a great deal in the reforming of life. Human nature is such that we soon become weary in well doing. We need more than an ideal—we need an inspiration. I like that phrase of Paul's ' The love of Christ constraineth us.' Constrain means to urge with irresistible power—that's the difference between copying a model and loving a personality. Love implies communion, and it is the communion which transforms. Mr. Weatherhead truly calls it a ' transforming friendship.'

CHAPTER VII

JESUS AND GOODNESS

WHAT DO WE MEAN BY GOODNESS?

IT is a queer fact of life that ugliness usually has a greater appeal than beauty !

Of course feminine beauty is nearly always attractive —even though it be the result of lipstick, pencil and powder ! But I'm not talking about the appeal of pretty girls in particular, but of the appeal of ugliness in general.

Take Hull Fair for example. This is one of the largest fairs in the country, and last year I had the opportunity of seeing it. What a queer, amusing, amazing affair it is ! It is a colossal collection of things unique, unusual and ugly. The smallest horse in the world and the largest dog are things unique. Motor cyclists who loop the loop in an iron cage are things unusual, and then, as the summit of sensationalism, you have Mary Ann Bevan—the ugliest woman on earth ! And people paid their precious pennies to go and see her. But, bless my soul, you needn't pay pennies to see ugliness : you can see it free any time you walk down the street ! What could you have uglier than rotten slums, city women who have sold their self-respect, or a drunken sot who has forfeited control of mind and body because he is too weak to control his thirst ?

Most of us take a morbid delight in things ugly.
We don't like to admit it, but it's true ! (That's why
scandal is so popular—people prefer to seek out the
sordid things about others, instead of the splendid
things !) Not only that ; think of the books that
have the biggest sale. Which are they ? Why, the
ones with the most filth in them ! The beauty of
English prose is neglected for the passing appeal of
passionate sex novels. Give a book an immodest
wrapper, and advertise it as ' hot stuff,' and it will
sell like ripe cherries ! We most of us have a secret
love of dirt, and will hover round it as flies hover round
a midden. And pure beauty goes unappreciated !

I once went to see a famous actor in a charming
little play called ' The Soul of Nicholas Sniders.'
It was a gem of literary beauty, and the acting was
superb. And yet there was only a handful of people
to witness it ! Those of us, however, who were there
clapped until the actor came before the curtain to make
a speech.

Thanking us for our applause, he regretted the fact
that there were so few people there to support him.
' If the play,' he said, ' had had lots of women kicking
their legs about, and a sprinkling of suggestive jokes,
the theatre would have been packed.'

I thought there was a profound pathos behind those
words. Good art is passed by while vulgarity and
ugliness win approval and applause. It has been the
same all through the ages. An ugly, dirty-minded
Emperor like Nero could rule an Empire, while the
best Man the world has ever known was spat on
and nailed to a cross !

Now, the fascination of the ugly partly explains the

general popularity of badness and the unpopularity of goodness ! Bad characters are often considered more interesting than good. It seems to be generally supposed that goodness is synonymous with dullness ! And that ' good people ' are frightfully tame and uninteresting.

A young lady once said to me, ' Oh, I don't like good people—they're so dull—I like folk with a bit of something about 'em ! ' And at the time, being young and ignorant, I agreed with her. (As a matter of fact, we were both young and ignorant—she was a flapper, and I was a youth of seventeen who was greatly thrilled and felt very big and important because I was walking a girl out !) But neither of us had learned to discriminate between goodness and goodie-goodieness—between piety and pharisaism !

When that flapper told me she didn't like good people she didn't really mean it. What she meant was that she didn't like goodie-goodie people ! Well, no more do I ! They make me squirm ! Goodie people are not really good but often repulsively bad. They are not charitable, courageous or pitiful. They have no real love, and they are not saints. They are often irritatingly mean and intolerant. They are not pious in the real sense of the word—they are Pharisees —and the Pharisees, as Studdert Kennedy once said, were to Jesus like a bad smell ! As a follower of Jesus Christ I test goodness by His standard, and according to Him *goodness* had nothing whatever to do with goodie-goodieness !

Now, let's try and get our thinking clear. We'll take two types of character and compare them.

First, I'll take an illustration from literature. In

the *Autobiography of Mark Rutherford* there is a description of a ministerial student who was a blonde youth with grey eyes, a mouth not quite shut, and an eternal simper on his face.   He was a great man at tea meetings, anniversaries and parties.   He was a fluent public speaker and dwelt much upon the joys of heaven and the possibility of meeting each other there.   He was close in money matters and when he left college the first thing he did was to marry a widow with a fortune.   He soon became a very popular minister in a town much visited by sick people with whom he was an exceptional favourite.

Now, keep that picture in mind and come with me into an engineering works.   We are in a workshop in which there are about fifty machines and mechanics. These men are not saints.   They swear, tell smutty yarns and gamble.   While the foreman is out of sight some of them begin to lark about with a coil of rope which they throw about the shop.   (Any kind of sky-larking is welcome as a relief to the day's monotony and they all join in the fun.)

Suddenly the rope catches in the cogs of a machine ; there is a grating and clanking and the machine is badly damaged.   The man who last threw the rope mutters a curse—he is a man with a wife and children, he stares at the broken machine as though stunned. He knows what it means—dismissal, and poverty for his children !

His mate, who is a single man, steals down the shop to the foreman's office.   A few minutes later he returns and patting the culprit on the back says, ' It's all right, J a k—I've seen the boss and told him I did it ! '

The other is amazed.

' Whatcher mean ? ' he asks.

' I mean this—you've a wife an' kids.   I ain't—see ?
If you're out o' work yer wife an' kids suffer.   Well—
I ain't no kids—so I told 'im I did it ! '

' Wot's 'e say ? '

' 'E cursed till 'e nearly bust—then 'e's gave me my
ticket and told me to 'op it.'

The two men shake hands, and before the culprit
can gather his wits together the other is gone.

That's from real life.   Now which do you call good ?
The pious parson described by Mark Rutherford or
the swearing mechanic ?   Which do you like the
better—the parson who preaches about heaven and
who panders to old ladies, or the man who swears and
sacrifices his job to save another from the sack ?   I
know which I like the better—the swearing mechanic—
not because of his swearing but because of his sacrifice.
And I think I know which Christ would like too.

That parson with his popularity, his pleasant
preaching and his wealthy widow wasn't good—he
was only goodie-goodie :   that is, his goodness was
superficial—it was just surface show—professional
piety !   And Jesus would have dealt with him as He
dealt with the Pharisees whom He called ' White-
washed sepulchres '—they may have looked white
and clean from the outside, but within there was
stinking death and rottenness.

Now, don't misunderstand me.   I'm not holding up
that mechanic as a saint—he was no more a saint
than a soda syphon is a sausage !   But he was nearer
Christ's ideal of goodness than the parson, because he
was unselfish.   He took the blame and lost his job
for the sake of a pal !   That pious parson was a selfish

prig. When I see a man of that description I want to kick him ! I'd rather hear a man swear than pretend to be pious and pander for popularity. It isn't religion, it's pretence and selfishness.

I don't want to be unjust to the poor little parson. I only want to be honest. It is quite probable that he really thought God liked him and listened to his eloquent sermons with the same interest as the old ladies did ! But whatever he thought, of this I'm certain, according to Jesus, God did not like him !

To be good according to Christian ideas is to live in the Spirit of Jesus. What is the Spirit of Jesus ? It is unselfishness ! God and duty first ! God's will above everything else, and my pals and others second, and myself and my own desires last—and a long way last ! That's the Christ Spirit !

How do these two fellows look in the light of that test ? How about the parson first ? Let's get down to his motives. What's he thinking about ? God ? Not he ! He's thinking about himself—number one ! Popularity first, then money—he feathers his own nest by marrying a wealthy widow. And then settles down to preach pleasant sermons about heaven to invalids and neurotics. He's not thinking of his duty or his pals—he's forgotten all about them ! His whole mind is filled with one idea—himself !

I don't want to be hard on the poor little fellow—I only want to be Christian. ' But,' you say, ' to be Christian is to be charitable ! ' To be Christian is to be Christ-like—and Christ said many fierce and hard things. He made it clear that we must put Him and duty before everything else. It may be hard, but it's Christian. That parson wasn't a Christian at all—he was *selfish*—and in Christ's eyes selfishness is sin. In fact, I'm inclined to think that that pious parson's preaching was more sinful than the mechanic's swearing.

Don't be shocked—I'm only trying to face the thing honestly without any humbug. I'm really asking this question—Which is worse, to profess piety and be a humbug ; or swear and be unselfish ? That mechanic fellow perhaps wasn't thinking of God, but he was certainly thinking of his pal. He may not have been a Christian—but he was certainly unselfish !

I wonder if you are beginning to see the difference between real goodness and just goodie-goodieness ? It isn't so much a question as to whether you go to church, wear black cloth and look solemn ; it isn't so much a question whether we believe the Thirty-Nine Articles or the Apostles Creed, and things like that—it's a question of your life-attitude towards God and your fellowmen. Do you love the Lord God with all your mind and strength, and your neighbour as yourself ? Real goodness isn't negative, it's positive ! It isn't just refraining from wrong—but positively doing right. It isn't just not telling lies, but definitely being honest. It isn't just not being immoral, but having a real hatred of lust and impurity—even in thought. It isn't just forgetting wrongs—but having a definite detestation of revenge, hatred, pride and selfishness !

In other words, real goodness is like the goodness of Christ, and He was neither dull, cowardly nor uninteresting. He was so brave, in fact, that He accepted the Cross rather than pander to popular taste ! He was so interesting that 2,000 years after His death men are still talking of Him and quarrelling about Him.

A man said to me the other day that he doesn't go to Church because there is so much controversy—so much quarrelling about creeds and so on. But don't you see that the very fact that there are so many people quarrelling about Jesus is proof of His uniqueness and power—people don't quarrel about things unless they consider them of vital importance !

Now, how about yourself ? It's always well to be personal in matters of this sort. I can imagine some saying to themselves something like this—' Um—well, I'm not such a bad sort. After all, I'm not a criminal or a thief ; I'm honest (at least people think so), I pay my bills, my weekly instalment for the motor-bike ; I don't beat my wife ; I don't swear (except to myself, when I hit my thumb with a hammer !), and I don't booze ! I'm a decent, clean-living chap ! '

Quite ! I'm prepared to accept all that. In fact, it's quite possible that you're a very fine person. I'm not so presumptuous as to call you a rotter or anything like that. But that isn't the point. The point is not whether you are decent, but whether you are the very best you can be !

During the War *John Bull* ridiculed an attempt the Churches made to call the Tommies to repentance, and Horatio Bottomley wrote : ' What right has the Church to talk to our splendid men about repentance ? They don't need repentance ; they are saints, every one of them ; to preach repentance to them is an insult.'

These words so amused one of the chaplains—the famous Woodbine Willie—that armed with a copy of *John Bull* he went among the men, and after flourishing it in front of them, read out an extract or two. Then.

closing it, he said, ' No, when Mr. Bottomley says you are splendid fellows I'm with him all the time. But when he says you are all saints—well, take a look at one another ! ' And the men roared with laughter. But behind that joke Woodbine Willie had hidden a tremendous thrust—and the men knew it ! They may have been very decent fellows. Most of them were, but they were far from what they ought to have been—and they knew it—and you know it, too !

Let me sketch you a word picture.

A back garden on a winter's day. Some newly-washed clothes hanging out to dry. Heavy clouds on the horizon form a dark background, and with the sun shining full on them the clothes look beautifully white. The clouds spread over the sky and snow begins to fall. Soon it is half-an-inch deep. Now the clothes on the line look dirty. Why ? Because in the first place with the sun shining on them and a dark background of clouds, and the green grass beneath, they looked white and clean in contrast to the dark surroundings. But now that the sun has gone and the dazzling white snow lies on the ground the clothes look dirty in contrast to the purity of the snow !

When we hang ourselves up in the garden of imagination with a good light on us and with some rough good-for-nothing fellows in the background, then we are tempted to think of ourselves as good and clean, but when we come up against a moral perfection like that of Jesus then we feel conscious of our own dirtiness.

A fisher fellow, who used to hang about the docks of an Eastern port many years ago, thought himself a really good chap. Then he got pally with a young carpenter, and eventually found the other so white that one day he knelt down at his feet and cried, ' Depart from me, for I am a sinful man, O Lord ! ' You and I may think ourselves good, but once we look at the snow-whiteness of the Christ we see ourselves, by contrast, to be unclean.

And that's all I want to say in this chapter—I just want, if I can, to lead you into the presence of Christ and let you for a moment behold the beauty of His face and feel those mercifully merciless eyes searching right down into the depths of your soul. Can you look straight into His eyes without having to lower your head ? I can't ! His purity is so dazzling white that I feel all dirty and wretched, and all I can do is to follow poor Peter's example and sink upon my knees and say, ' Depart from me, for I am a sinful man.'

So you see, when I talk about goodness, I really mean 'Christ-likeness.' Now, how about having a 'go' at that Christ-likeness ? If I ask a cabinet-maker to make me a piece of furniture and he's a genuine workman and not a slacker, he'll do that piece of work as well as ever he can. And if I say to him, ' My word, that's a fine piece of work ! ' all he will say is ' Bless my soul, if a thing's worth doing, it's worth doing well!' Of course it is ! And if life's worth living, it's worth living well. We might as well live as well as we possibly can. That's the whole point of this chapter —I want to make you face up to life, look at it straight in the eyes, and then resolve to make it the best you can—don't be content with jerry work in the building of character.

Don't forget you are, to a great extent, the captain of your soul—there are in you great possibilities—

possibilities for good or evil—you can be mean or you can be mighty, you can crawl in the slime, or you can climb to the summits, you can be grovelling or you can be great—saint or sinner. And it all depends upon your own choice; Christ—or the line of least resistance—which has a downward slope!

In one of Studdert Kennedy's poems a soldier in the trenches muses thus—

> I'm a man, and a man's a mixture,
> Right down from 'is very birth,
> For part of 'im comes from 'Eaven,
> An' part of 'im comes from Earth.
> There's nothin' in man that's perfect,
> And nothin' that's all complete,
> 'E's nobbut a big beginning,
> From 'is 'ead to the soles of 'is feet,
> There's summat as draws 'im uppards,
> An' summat as drags 'im down,
> And the consequence is 'e wobbles,
> Twixt muck and a golden crown.

Which is it to be?—The muck or the golden crown? Are you going to give way to the downward pull, or strive to respond to the upward urge? Have you ever faced up to the question before? If not, I want you to face up to it now—just stop reading a minute and think.

What are you doing with life? Just muddling along, any old how, or are you making of it a thing of beauty and nobility. That Perfect Christ who trod the road of Galilee comes to you searching your heart with His beautiful eyes and beckoning you with His nail-pierced hands to follow Him. Will you follow? Will you give yourself to that Christ to try and live His way? Are you ready to take Him as your pattern of goodness, as your teacher and guide? Surrender to Him as the ideal. That's how Thomas began—the travelling preacher of Galilee was His ideal—but there came a time when He was more than that—and Thomas cried, 'My Lord and my God!'

And that experience of Thomas's has been repeated millions of times since. That has been my experience. I began with the human Jesus—surrendered to Him as Guide—but I soon found that He was more than human, that He was divine. That He was not only a Guide to Goodness, but that He was the Source of Goodness—Goodness itself! God! And with Thomas I now kneel down and cry, 'My Lord and my God!'

Will you kneel with me? And make this poem a prayer:

> Give me the man-soul, God-pure, brave, serene,
>   To meet these days.
> Ready to walk, head high, with firm, sure tread,
>   My life's strange ways.
>
> I would be soul-poised, great in gentleness,
>   Gentle in power,
> Rich in self-giving, pouring life and love
>   Into each hour.
>
> Help me to sing and fight, not weep and cower
>   When blows fall fast:
> Patient to bear, strong to endure—thy son,
>   True to the last.
>
> Let me live grandly, seek the things that last,
>   Press toward love's goal;
> Win jewels? fame?—nay, better, when earth's past
>   Stand a crownéd soul.
>
> So be my helper, Father, comfort me
>   With staff and rod,
> Till I shall give Thee back my life well lived
>   For man and God.

CHAPTER VIII

JESUS AND CHEER

Is Religion Dull?

HAVE you ever thought what an important part of your anatomy your face is? Your face is like the ' pressure gauge ' on a boiler. To change the metaphor, your face is the barometer by which other people can see what climatic conditions prevail in that little kingdom called ' you.' When you look surly people think : ' Oh—there's a deep depression there. Further outlook unsettled ' . . . and so they move on to sunnier climes !

And have you ever thought what a difference your mouth makes to your face? Wouldn't you look funny without a mouth? And have you ever thought what a difference your mouth can make to your expression? Here's a little experiment for you : Draw three circles on a bit of paper. In the top half of each circle make two dots for eyes, and, in the middle, one dot for the nose. Then, in the first circle, draw a short straight horizontal line—that's the mouth, and a mouth with little expression. In the next circle draw the mouth by making an inverted semi-circle (like a horse-shoe held upside down with all the good luck run out of it) that's a mouth with the corners turned down—Dismal Dick's mouth ! Then, in the third circle, turn the horse-shoe the other way up, like a half moon on its back—that's a mouth with the corners turned up, the mouth of a Cheerful Charlie.

That little experiment will just show what a difference your mouth can make to the expression on your face.

In the *Daily Express* some time ago there appeared an article with the striking title ' Your face in 1931—what will you make of it ? ' The writer suggested that discontented faces are the most common. I'm rather inclined to think they are. The inverted-horse-shoe-type-of-mouth is seen only too often. Judging by people's faces one would suppose, as Mr. H. Casson has pointed out, that the largest association in Great Britain is the National Gloom Association.

Have you ever met members of the N.G.A. ? I suppose you have. They're really terrible people to meet. They believe that happiness is bad form ; they consider laughter a breach of decorum ; and when they see any one smile they consider it a sign of mental weakness. I am told that every member of the N.G.A. signs this pledge—

> *I hereby solemnly promise to abstain from all outward demonstrations of amusement, and from all gaiety and frivolity.*

You can always find plenty of these Dismal Dicks about—they always look as though they're sucking lemons !

' But,' I can imagine my readers thinking, ' we cannot help our faces ! ' No, we cannot—but we can make the best of a bad job ! That reminds me of a story I heard of a little girl who received a present of a Teddy Bear. Unfortunately one of its eyes was injured in the post. Asked what name she had given it the child said : ' I call it Gladly, because I read in a book the other day : " Gladly my cross I'd bear." ' She was making the best of a bad job.

When you meet these Dismal Dicks and ask them how they are they say, ' Fair.' Ask how things are going : ' Moderate.' And how's business ? ' Rotten.' To them business is always bad and the country is everlastingly on the way to the dogs. No wonder they find business bad ! I patronize shops where I get cheerful service.

The trouble is that many people expect to get everything out of life without putting anything into it. Lots of youths, for instance, seem to think that they ought to begin where their fathers left off, and then, when they find there's no easy road to fame, they sulk —give up trying, and wonder why Fortune doesn't smile on them. The wife who has expected a thorough Prince Charming, and has only found a nice, difficult, ordinary man, is gnawed with discontent until she acquires a face that would drive any sane husband straight into another woman's arms.

It generally happens that you get out of life about as much as you put into it. ' Whatsoever a man soweth, that shall he also reap.' Sow smiles, and you'll probably reap smiles ; look daggers at Mrs. Jinks and she'll probably look bayonets at you !

Now, I am going to marshal the rest of my remarks under three headings : (1) The Evil of Gloom ; (2) The Value of Cheer ; (3) The Cheer of Christ.

First then : *The Evil of Gloom*. I consider gloom a sin. I don't think God ever intended us to be miserable. I think it is just as wrong to spread sadness as it is to spread badness. I'll tell you why. Gloom causes bad health. Most people know that their emotions affect their bodies. The emotion of rage, for instance, raises the blood pressure.

Take, as an outstanding example, the effect of fear. Have you ever seen any one really afraid ? And did you notice how the fear affected the body ? This is what happens to the body of one who is afraid. The eyes and mouth open widely, and the eyebrows are raised. The frightened person at first stands like a statue—motionless and breathless. Then his heart begins to beat violently, the skin becomes pale, perspiration exudes from it (and the remarkable thing is that the surface of the skin is cold—hence the expression a ' cold sweat '). The hair on the skin stands erect, the salivary glands act imperfectly, the mouth becomes dry and the voice husky, &c., &c.

I've told you all that to show how the emotions— which are mental—affect the body, which is physical. Your mind has a tremendous power over your body. Well then, what effect has gloom on the body ? It has a distinctly bad effect. Doctors tell us that sorrow affects one's health to such an extent that people even die of it. You've perhaps heard people say ' she died of a broken heart.' And it's quite true, sorrow does kill. I know a lady who is lying on an invalid's bed now. She has been there for years. And it is simply sorrow that has brought her there— her son is what we usually call ' a bad lot '; and her grief is slowly killing her.

Well then, if sorrow and gloom have such an evil effect on one's health and general condition, it is perfectly obvious that to spread sorrow is a sin—it is a sin against society because it destroys society's well-being. Not only so, but sorrow and sadness are bad (as I have pointed out) for commerce. And they are fearfully bad for the Church.

What a lot of Dismal Dicks and Doleful Desmonds I've found in churches. (Some churches seem to be regular breeding grounds for 'em.) You've met them I suppose—they are always asking what the world is coming to : to them, modern young people are a thoroughly bad lot, they consider all beauty of form and sound and colour of the Devil ; to go to a place of amusement is to be on the road to hell ; and, of course, things are never what they were.

I've come out of some so-called Christian homes after half an hour's conversation, feeling utterly despondent, depressed and dejected ; with my faith in human nature shaken, all my hopes smashed, and my optimism shattered . . . and I've just felt I've wanted to put my head in my hands and weep. And then, half an hour after—when I've pulled myself together again—I've felt like going back and pushing all those so-called Christian heads into the copper and putting the fire on and giving 'em a good boiling !

Oh, gentle reader, if ever the parson comes to your house (and you want him to come again) for goodness sake don't start the doleful ditty business because, if you do, he'll not want to come again. He spends half his life listening to people's tales of woe.

Of course if you're in real trouble or bereaved or

in difficulty it's different—but under normal conditions, for goodness sake smile.

> What's the use of grumbling,
> It never was worth while.
> So pack up your troubles
> In your old kit bag
> And smile ! smile ! smile !

I once went to see a dear old lady who was in great trouble, she said : ' I must be brave and bear it ! ' And then she changed the conversation and actually smiled—smiled through her tears. Oh, I did admire that. That's what I call courage. Why, there are some folks who grumble and grouse over the slightest inconveniences. But that old lady had had enough trouble in her life to turn most of us insane. And she had the courage to smile through her tears.

Do you think Christ would make you feel depressed if He were to come to your home ? I'm certain He wouldn't. He'd fill you with hope and courage as He did His disciples ! Be of good cheer ! So much then, for the Evil of Gloom.

Now for *The Value of Cheer*. I was reading a book [1] a little time ago in which the author told how once he was in a nursing home, all bandaged up and out of order. One day he was listening in on the wireless. Suddenly John Henry—the Yorkshire comedian—was put on. And the writer said : ' It was all good natural fun, and I laughed so hard that I nearly burst my bandages. Laugh ! Didn't I laugh ! It was worth all the hygiene and surgery put together. If ever I'm about to die I'll ask to listen in to John Henry on the wireless and I'll laugh myself alive again ! '

[1] *Looking on the Bright Side*. H. N. Casson.

So you see, just as gloom leads to bad health, so joy leads to good health. Laughter is the best cure for every trouble, insomnia and melancholia. It's an aid to digestion, and the best sauce for any dinner.

Have you ever realized that comedians are as valuable to society as doctors and nurses ? They are. If there were no comedians and humorists to make us laugh we'd all be neurotics or lunatics.

Think how terrible it would be trying to put up with our next door neighbour if we never saw the funny side of things ! Why, we'd all be murdering each other ! You know, we're all a bit queer when you come to think of it, and we must be terribly annoying to our friends. But they just smile at our little ways and overlook them. Have you ever looked at your reflection in a mirror and thought how funny you are ? I once caught a glimpse of myself in a mirror un-expectedly—and I got such a surprise. I'd never realized that I looked funny before. And at first it made me want to weep for shame. And then the humour of it struck me—and I laughed at myself— and the more I laughed the funnier I looked, and the funnier I looked the more I laughed, until at last I'd to drag myself away from the mirror before it broke. I'm sure if I were to meet myself walking down the street I should die of laughing.

Yes, laughter helps to keep us healthy and sane, it makes human relationships tolerable, it is good for business : and, if only we would learn to laugh more, we should quarrel less. Many a strike could have been prevented by a good hearty laugh.

Laughter, too, is a great educational force. Just as you often can get a child to take a pill when it is wrapped up in a spoonful of jam, so you can get people to accept a truth when it is wrapped up in a spoonful of humour. Any orator of experience knows that laughter is his best ally. A crowd often can be made to laugh itself into agreement or enthusiasm. That's why I sometimes make jokes in sermons—some people think I'm irreverent. I'm not. When I took up preaching seriously, I thought to myself : ' Now, I've got to find out the best way of getting truths across into the minds of the crowds.' And so I began studying the methods of all successful orators. If any one could get a crowd and hold it, then I wanted to know how it was done. I listened to stump orators at street corners, cheap jacks on the markets, Salvation Army officers, politicians, famous preachers and so on. And I noticed that the men with the biggest crowds, the men who were successful in selling their goods, or winning converts or votes—or whatever it was they wanted to do—were the men who could crack a joke and appreciate a laugh. And I thought, why, bless my life, the reason why people don't like sermons is that they are usually so dull. And why should they be dull ? Christianity is the most optimistic, hopeful and joyful philosophy in the world. Its keynote is cheer—' be of good cheer '—and so I began to try and brighten up my sermons a bit. I believe in making sermons more palatable by sometimes serving them up with a little fun sauce.

A story is told of the late Sir George Reid, Premier of Australia, to the effect that once he was faced by a crowd which was opposed to his policy. As soon as he began to talk he was interrupted by a heckler, who yelled—' George, you've got two faces ! '

And Sir George replied : ' I expect you've only got one, or you wouldn't be wearing the one you have.'

The crowd roared, and from that moment Sir George had them as clay in his hands.

And now for *The Cheer of Christ*. I have usually found, in conversation with men of the world, that they consider Christians to be people with long faces and gloomy dispositions !

I am afraid that many of these queer ideas about Christians are due to the influence of the pictures one often sees of the Christ as the Man of Sorrows. It is true, Jesus was called ' the Man of Sorrows,' but I feel sure he was also a *Man of Joy*.

Have you ever met people, who, in the midst of their trouble, still kept radiant in spirit, and whose eyes still shone with a glad serenity which no sorrow in the world could dispel ? That's what I think Christ was like. He had His troubles—

> Anguish that made pale the sun.

But He smiled through His tears.

I once read the Gospels through to discover for myself what sort of a man Jesus really was. And I came to the conclusion that He had a very fine sense of humour, and that He even made jokes in his sermons.

Here's one example. You will remember that Jesus once told a story of a man who was in bed when a neighbour came at midnight pestering him for a loaf of bread. Just try and imagine the scene—this is the vision the story would suggest to the minds of the people to whom it was told. The house consists of one square room, like a large square box. There is no chimney and the place is stuffy and smoky. The floor is just hard baked clay. In the middle of the floor is a fire—like a camp fire. All the family sleep in the same room. They don't undress—they just spread out their sleeping mats on the floor and arrange themselves like the spokes of a wheel all radiating from the fire with their feet near to it. (In winter the fire is kept alight all night.)

Well, this poor fellow is just going off to sleep when there comes a frightful knocking at the door.

' Who's there ? ' he cries.

' It's me ! ' the voice responds.

' I know it's you. But who are you? What do you want?—go away.'

Still the knocking.

' What do you want ? '

' Bread.'

I leave you to imagine the rest of the conversation —it wouldn't be too polite.

Then the exasperated man in the house says : ' Oh, bother you—I'm in bed with my children and can't come.'

Can't you imagine the crowd roaring with laughter at that ? You see, the poor fellow would have to tread carefully and pick his way over all the sleeping members of the family to get to the pantry. And then he'd have to step carefully over several more—his wife included—to get to the door. And the opening of the door would make a draught and he'd be desperately afraid of wakening his wife and so getting a curtain lecture for his trouble.

But the man at the door makes such a noise that in sheer desperation the father says : if only he will stop making that unholy noise—which may wake the baby any minute—he'll give him the whole of the house ! ! !

Don't you appreciate the humour of the story ? I'm sure Jesus meant the people to laugh at it. And I think they did—it says : ' They heard him *gladly*.' It wouldn't say that if the crowds sat looking as glum as I've seen some crowds listening to sermons.

Now, this is where you and I come in. Have we got this cheerful brand of Christianity which I've been advocating ? I believe this is the only genuine brand— the brand with a smiling face as its label. Do people kindle at your radiant personality ? Do they warm their starved souls at the glow of your spirit ? Do they feel braver and better because they have met you ?

It was said on one occasion as Phillips Brooks was coming down the aisle after preaching one of his wonderful sermons, a working man nudged his mate and said : ' Bill, it makes you feel good just to look at him.'

I wish I'd got a radiance like that, don't you ? How can we get such a Christ-like radiance ?

(1) First, we must experience the Forgiveness of Sins in Christ. We have all sinned, even the best of us, and we need God's forgiveness. And Christ is saying to all who are truly penitent : ' Thy sins which are many, are forgiven.' That's something to rejoice over, isn't it ?

You remember the joy that came to Saul Kane, the scoundrel, in Masefield's Poem, ' The Everlasting Mercy ' ? Let me refresh your memory. Saul Kane has just been converted and he exclaims :

O glory of the lighted mind.
How dead I'd been, how dumb, how blind.
The station brook, to my new eyes,

Was babbling out of Paradise,
The waters rushing from the rain
Were singing Christ has risen again.
I thought all earthly creatures knelt
For rapture of the joy I felt.
The narrow station-wall's brick ledge,
The wild hop withering in the hedge,
The lights in huntsman's upper story,
Were parts of an eternal glory,
Were God's eternal garden flowers.
I stood in bliss at this for hours.

First, then, we must experience the rapture that comes of the forgiveness of sins in Christ.

(2) Secondly, we must learn to renounce ourselves. Selfishness is the greatest gloom manufacturer there is. If we wish to be really happy, with a deep peace in our hearts, we must seek only to do God's will. We must see God's will in the job we are doing every day. (If it cannot be reconciled with God's will we must get out of it.) We must get away from the idea that one only does God's will when one lives in a monastery, or sits in a church and sings hymns. I don't think it is God's will that men and women should stifle all their affection, and shut out all the charm of life by living within the walls of monasteries and convents. Our life-work should be service to the community, and when we work in the service of our fellow men we work to the Glory of God.

Work shall be prayer, if all be wrought
    As Thou wouldst have it done ;
And prayer, by Thee inspired and taught,
    Itself with work be one.

Remember, if you are a grocer, and are selling real wholesome food instead of cheap imitations, then you are doing something to answer the prayers of those who say : ' Give us this day our daily bread.' If we are really living according to God's will we shall experience the peace that passeth understanding.

(3)   And lastly, if we are certain of God—as certain of God as Jesus was—then we have a secret source of strength and hope that nothing can shatter. If pain comes, we can pray—' Let me fight and win if I can ; and if not, wrest from it something splendid, something that will make my character nobler. If disaster comes let me face it bravely as Christ faced the Cross.'

> When anxious cares would break my rest,
> And griefs would tear my throbbing breast,
> Thy tuneful praises, raised on high,
> Shall check the murmur and the sigh.

I believe we disappoint Christ if we fail to enter into the heritage of over-bubbling delight, of the sheer joy of life that He has made possible for us. ' Be of good cheer.' Be radiant. And you cannot have this radiance—real lasting radiance—without these three sources any more than you can have a reservoir of life-giving water without the streams which come down from the hills to feed it.

And now abideth these three sources—the joy that comes of the forgiveness of sins ; the joy of working together with God to do His will and serve humanity ; and the joy that comes of the certainty of God. And the greatest of these is the certainty of God.

If we will give ourselves entirely to Him, then we shall be able to sing—

> For sorrow and sadness I joy shall receive,
> And share in the gladness of all that believe.

CHAPTER IX

JESUS AND PLEASURE

Is Pleasure the End and Aim of Life?

THERE is a film with the title ' Children of Pleasure.' Crowds of people to-day are purely and simply ' Children of Pleasure.' They just make pleasure their philosophy—it is the aim and end of their existence. To be happy, to have a good time, to satisfy desires, appetites and passions, seems to be their sole purpose in life.

You remember how this is expressed in the poem Omar Khayyam?

Look to the Rose that blows about us—' Lo,'
' Laughing,' she says : ' Into the world I blow :
At once the silken Tassel of my purse
Tear, and its Treasure on the Garden throw.'

The Worldly Hope men set their Hearts upon
Turns Ashes—or it prospers ; and anon,
Like snow upon the Desert's dusty Face
Lighting a little Hour or two—is gone.

Ah, my Beloved, fill the Cup that clears
To-day of past regrets and future Fears—
To-morrow ?—Why, To-morrow I may be
Myself with Yesterday's Sev'n Thousand Years.

Lo ! Some we loved, the loveliest and the best
That time and Fate of all their Vintage prest,
Have drunk their Cup a round or two before,
And one by one crept silently to Rest.

And we, that now make merry in the Room
They left, and Summer dresses in new Bloom,
Ourselves must we beneath the Couch of Earth
Descend, ourselves to make a Couch—for whom?

Ah, make the most of what we yet may spend,
Before we too into the dust descend;
Dust into Dust, and under Dust, to lie,
Sans Wine, Sans Song, Sans Singer, and—Sans End.

That's how many people think. And, it must be admitted, I've often been tempted to adopt a similar point of view. When hopes have been shattered, and the Castle of Dreams one has been busy building for years has come with a crash to the ground, and, ' Some we loved—the loveliest and the best '—have drunk their Cup a round or two, and then ' crept silently to Rest '—it makes you feel very uncertain of everything . . . God ! . . . And a Purpose ruling Life ! . . . Immortality ! . . . What are these things ? Vain imaginings ? . . . Futile hopes ? Childish dreams ? . . . Who can tell ?

Oh, come with old Khayyam, and leave the Wise
To talk; one thing is certain, that life flies;
One thing is certain, and the rest is Lies.

So, ' Make the most of what we yet may spend ' —make the best of a bad job—have a good time—do as the Tommies did in the War, ' Pack up your troubles and smile '—smile in the face of fate—don't stop to think—drink the cup to the dregs—' Eat, drink and be merry, for to-morrow—to-morrow we may be dead, and once we are dead, we are dead for a long time.'

Have you never felt like that ? I have—often. And when I felt like that it wasn't much use a pious person coming to me and saying : ' My dear fellow, you mustn't think like that—it's blasphemy ! We cannot understand God's inscrutable purpose, but we must have faith and trust Him when we cannot see.'

That sort of talk only makes me angry. I hate goodie-goodie piety and sanctimonious sentiment. I like to know the reason for things. I should make a bad soldier—that idea of

> Theirs not to reason why,
> Theirs but to do and die,

wouldn't have suited me. I always have wanted to know the ' reason why.'

Well then, if Christianity says that to make Pleasure the aim and end of life is wrong, then I want to know why it's wrong. Why is it wrong ?

Let's begin with ourselves. Here we are—you and I : funny little animals walking on two legs, wearing tight shoes, and dressing up in our plus fours or tight skirts to make ourselves look smart ; painting our lips and powdering our noses ; shaving our chins or oiling our hair ; each fretting his little time upon the stage—eating and drinking, sleeping and waking, working and playing, loving and hating, joying and sorrowing.

And we each of us have in our personalities those queer animal peculiarities—instincts, passions, appetites : and they can be blesséd or blasting ! And we all live together—' And the more we are together the happier we shall be,' we sing. And we are all dependent upon one another—the butcher, the baker, and the candlestick-maker, the tinker,

tailor, soldier, sailor, rich man, poor man—all except
the beggar man and thief are of great importance.

And we are valuable to one another—or ' Society '
as we call it—only if we learn to conform to certain
standards of conduct.   And those standards of conduct
are thousands of years old—and we call them the
Ten Commandments.   And we pay policemen to see
that they are obeyed, and barristers, and solicitors,
and lawyers and similar queer fry to argue about
them.   And now, in this age of rush and hurry, when we
cut everything as short as we can—when we write short
letters, ask for short sermons, go short cuts, and wear
short jackets and short skirts—we have cut the
Commandments short, so short in fact, that we have
only three left.   They are (1) Thou shalt not kill ;
(2) Thou shalt not commit adultery ; (3) Thou shalt
not steal. (During the War we knocked the NOT
out of all three.   You couldn't have a war unless you
did that.   But we've put it back again now.)

And we observe these three remaining Commandments because life would be utterly intolerable if we
didn't.   If we didn't obey these three Commandments,
life would permanently be as it was in the war—human
life would be cheap, and murder winked at ; the sacredness of sex relationships violated, and no one's
property safe.

You see, if one man kills another, he's a bit of a
nuisance.   Even if the person he killed is a thoroughly
bad lot, yet the murderer is a somewhat unnerving
person to have at large !   You see, he may some day
make up his mind to kill *you* or *me*.   And so, to make
ourselves safe we deprive him of life.   We say : the
law says ' Thou shalt not kill,' and so, because you've

killed someone else, we are going to kill you.   (It's a bit inconsistent, but that's how it works.)   ' Thou shalt not kill.'

Again, if one man will persist in making love to another man's wife, it's going to make things impossible. And, if we didn't consider the marriage ties sacred, what would happen to the children ?   The State would have to look after them, because home-life, as we know it, would disappear.   That's why that middle Commandment is so important.   ' Thou shalt not commit adultery.'

And if the milkman were to walk into the grocer's shop, and help himself to a rasher of ham, without paying for it ;   or, if the window-cleaner were to become a cat burglar and steal the milkman's wife's jewelry— well, that would all be awkward and confusing too ! And so, to prevent such things happening, we still keep the last of those three Commandments, and we employ a force of well-built men, and trust them to keep a look-out for any unusual conduct.

Well then.   What's it all got to do with Pleasure ? Pleasure is the satisfaction, or gratification, of our appetites, passions, and instincts.   And when we seek to satisfy our appetites, passions, and instincts, we have to be very careful, because it is quite probable that we shall break one, or all three, of these remaining Commandments.

Take *Instinct* for example.   One of the most powerful instincts is that of self-preservation.   There's something within which urges us to keep alive at all costs.   If someone attacks us, that ' something ' makes us either fight for all we are worth, or turn tail and run for dear life.   If we are hungry, then that instinct urges us to get hold of food. Instinct doesn't mind *how* we get it—we can beg, borrow or steal, for all Instinct cares—all it says is ' get it ' by hook or by crook ! Satisfy your hunger ! And, of course, if we follow the dictates of instinct, and get food, and don't pay for it, then we break that Commandment which says : ' Thou shalt not steal.'

But the instinct of self-preservation is not the only one that demands satisfaction. There are crowds of others—and one of the most powerful is the instinct of self-perpetuation—the sex instinct. And if we are not extremely careful, this instinct will make us break the Commandment which says : ' Thou shalt not commit adultery.'

And then there is Passion, or strong feeling. We all of us have waves of passion surging through us, like storms coming down from the hills, and sweeping through a valley. There are the passions of Love, Hate, Resentment and so forth. Passion's a queer thing—half the murders and suicides are due to it.

Tommy Jones may be quite a decent, normal creature. One day, entering a strange room, he sees a strange girl. Something in that girl's personality stirs something in his personality. He suddenly becomes mentally unbalanced. His blood pressure goes up, his heart begins thumping at his ribs like a prisoner hammering at the door of his cell. He becomes excited, and after the parting he can think of nothing but that girl—but why describe it all ? you've most of you gone through it at some time or other ! In other words, Passion has taken possession of him— the Passion of Love. And supposing he sees someone insult that girl—it's like a red rag to a bull; he's all rage and indignation, and if he isn't very careful he'll strike that other fellow, and perhaps kill him. So, before you know where you are, the other Commandment is broken—'Thou shalt not kill.' So you see, you have to be extremely careful. That's why I say these instincts, passions and appetites can be blesséd or blasting. That's all another way of saying that to make human life tolerable we must have *control* over our instincts, appetites and passions. We all of us start life, as it were, with a bundle of tendencies—these tendencies can make or mar us— it all depends upon whether they are used or abused. The people who use their tendencies properly develop what we usually term 'CHARACTER'—meaning, of course, good character. This high quality character is of the first importance—it matters more than Acts of Parliament. It is the greatest thing in life. A good character is an asset to the human race, and a bad one is a liability.

Well then, we have seen, quite apart from religion, that we are only of value to one another—or Society— if we develop good characters. Does Pleasure make for Good Character? In moderation it plays its part. But in excess it destroys.

Don't misunderstand me. I am not saying that all pleasure is wrong. Pleasure, most certainly, has an important place in life. It is *excessive* pleasure— making the pursuit of happiness the aim and end of life—which is wrong. When you only do the things you want to do, or like to do: the things which bring pleasant sensations; you become weak and valueless. A footballer couldn't keep fit on chocolate creams and

Turkish delight. And you can't keep a character good and strong on the sweets of life.

Now look at it another way. Jesus once said : ' By their fruits ye shall know them.' That's always a final test. By their fruits — by their results ye shall test their value. What are the results of this Pleasure Philosophy ? They are—mental dejection, physical disease, and moral degradation for the individual. And inevitable decay for society.

Let's look at that closer. Here's a youth—a nice lad—only about nineteen, with a strong healthy body, and a gay sunny disposition.

' O you old sober sides,' he cries, ' you miserable, mournful, mumbling ministers give me the pip. I'm going to enjoy life—have a good time—one's only young once.'

' But,' we protest, ' do be careful.'

' Oh ! that's all right,' he says. ' Cheer up—I can look after myself all right."

And so we leave him. He's not bad. He's a tophole fellow, and we can't help but like him. He's reckless, that's all.

But see the picture later. His health and high spirits have gone, his body is frail, his nerves shattered. He's lost his job. He's without money and friends. A shipwrecked soul.

Men have sometimes said to me : ' My dear chap, a fellow must sow his wild oats.' Well, if a man must sow his wild oats he will have to reap a wild harvest. ' Whatsoever a man soweth that shall he also reap.' That's the natural law, the inevitable sequence—and there's no escape from it. You can no more alter that than you can prevent the tide coming in.

The writer of a book I was reading the other day said: ' I wish all young men could read a letter I have before me. It is written by a youth who has strayed from the path of purity and is now suffering the very torture of hell, with a broken spirit, a despairing heart, and a weakened body. He asks: "Is there any hope for me?" He has been driven to the very verge of suicide. This is the bitter harvest of suffering and degradation which follows the sowing of wild oats.'

I believe in having a fence at the top of the cliff, not an ambulance at the bottom—that's why I'm writing like this. I could tell you of men who have come to me—men who have been big and strong, soldiers some of them—and kneeling before me they have wept like children. Their nerves have been wasted, their homes ruined, and other lives blasted . . . and they have hated themselves, they've cried in an agony of shame—cried because of the ruin they have made of life. And they've told me they never intended to end like that. It was all so simple—they just wanted a ' good time.' If you stop rowing a boat and just drift, you'll probably drift to the rapids. These men didn't deliberately set out for hell, but they lost their way to heaven.

I've just been reading the story of an American grocer who was so busy making money that he didn't notice a tragedy being staged right under his very nose in his own home. Eventually things came to a head. The fellow's wife (who was one of those ' arty arty ' sort of people, who substitute literature and art for morality and religion, and who talk about ' art for art's sake ' and all that sort of tosh) fell in love with an author. Their daughter was friendly with a boy called Jack. Their friendship was of the platonic variety. They were just two healthy, gay, spirited, young things, who laughed at religion as out of date, and had their own ideas of morality.

One day this girl discovered her mother being embraced by the author fellow. She was stunned. Her mother ! Her mother—whom she had thought so different. Why should *she* strive to keep herself above reproach when her own mother was acting like that ? What was the use ? What was the use of anything ? She decided to let go.

A short time after she arranged a party. Alcohol was smuggled into a club, and she and her pals painted the night red. By midnight they were most of them fairly tight, and amid much excitement they packed themselves into motor-cars and dashed off into the country. And the driver of the last car was so intoxicated that he lost control. The car dashed over a cliff, and he was killed.

You can imagine the climax of it all ! The whole story of the drunken party came to light. The parents of the dead boy were disgraced. The grocer's daughter was involved and his reputation was dragged in the mud. The affair between the grocer's wife and the author came to light, and the grocer vowed to kill him. The smuggler of the alcohol was involved, his family was disgraced. In short, crowds of people were affected by the action of one.

And this is the point. All that tangled tragedy was the result of irreligion. It was the result of that pernicious modern doctrine of ' Please yourself and have a jolly good time.'

Later in the book, in conversation with a friend, the

grocer is made to say : ' My wife is not a bad woman, my daughter is not a bad girl. They have simply lost their grip on the realities of life. They are seeing things out of proportion. Religion is not for them a living force. Therefore, they have turned to other interests—interests which in themselves have not the character-sustaining power of the Christianity of Jesus.'

I am convinced that there you have the explanation of many modern shipwrecks—wrecked homes and wrecked lives. Religion is left out. These people have no God—and they end in tragedy, and wonder why.

Christianity is the greatest and most effective character-sustaining power there is. Psychology may tell you how your instincts and appetites may be controlled. But it doesn't actually help you as religion does. I've read about as much psychology as most people, and when I've done a thing I can usually explain the motives that prompted me to do it. But psychology doesn't keep me straight. It leaves me crying out : ' What I would not that I do.' Art is the same. It teaches me how to appreciate beauty with my senses—but it doesn't help me to control my passions.

So many of us moderns like to think we are advanced —we've got science, culture, intellectuality, art and so on. There is a type of modern youth which scoffs at religion as out of date. It laughs at morality and the sacredness of the marriage ties. Marriage—and love—it was all right in our grandmothers' time. But it's different now—marriage for keeps is bunk— it's obsolete.

These young intellectuals wear their hair in weird fashions, smoke innumerable cigarettes, attend plays and read novels which would have shocked their grandparents, sit in Bohemian lounges discussing intimate and sacred things in quite a glib irreverent way. 'Let's be honest with ourselves,' they say. 'We are free—we've got instincts, let's follow 'em.'

In a modern play an old window cleaner keeps on saying: 'Wot oi say is—foller yer instincts.' And that seems to sum up the philosophy of many people to-day. They just follow instinct. But our instincts, although very valuable and powerful, like everything else must be guarded and controlled. Water is good. Without it all life would cease. But a great flood is destructive. Our instincts are good. But whole nations have been destroyed by instincts when they have been loosed beyond control. And to keep instincts under control and make them a blessing rather than a curse, God has given us religion. Whenever in history the spiritual has been banished, licentiousness has ruled, and ruin has followed.

Christianity has been scoffed at and mocked at throughout the ages. There are still those who mock at it. But mock as you like, it is the only thing that I know which can keep your life stable and wholesome. To try to fight your lower instincts by sheer force of will may be possible to some, but with most of us it is a hopeless task. Within the limits of your kitchen grate your fire is a welcome and useful thing. But let its sparks get beyond the grate and set your furniture ablaze—then it is a thing of terror and power—merciless, destructive, devastating.

Your instincts, appetites and passions are like that. Religion is the grate, as it were, which keeps them in control. But once let them get a grip on the household of life, and they are as merciless, destructive and devastating as the fire.

Just a word in conclusion. I know what some of you are up against. I've had the valuable experience of working in both a factory and an office. And I know the kind of thing that goes on. The happy-go-lucky morality which sees no guilt in sin and no merit in virtue. I know the contempt of things religious and the predominance of smut in the day's conversation. And I know too that girls are as bad as fellows—that often a pretty face is the index to a very mean and dirty little soul. Now, if the fellows and girls who read my words want to keep their characters clean, and make life worth while, and of value to society, they must fight. There is in me

> That underworld where lust and lies
>   Like vermin crawl and creep
> Across my visions and my prayers
>   Whence sordid passions leap.
>
> To slay the very thing I love,
>   To crucify my Lord,
> And force me spit my sins upon
>   The face my soul adores. [1]

You've got to set your teeth and clench your fists and turn your back on the rottenness, the stink and slime of things. And you'll not succeed if you trust entirely to your own strength—good resolutions won't stand the test of city temptations ; and philosophy is no match for passion. The environments of life make it easy to do wrong and hard to do right. And when some men discover this their courage fails and they let go and sink. That's the result of leaving God out.

[1] Studdert Kennedy.

You've no doubt seen ships in a river swinging with the tide and seeming as if to follow it out to sea ; and yet they remained in position because, down below the waves, the anchor held them fast. You need an anchor to hold you secure against the tides of temptation. There's that in all of us that would rather let go than hold on. I know the intense and appalling difficulty of the road up, and yet, I know with a thrill, that there is redemption in Jesus' goodness, and that He can break the grip of the beast and lift me up and sustain me.

> He breaks the power of cancelled sin,
>   He sets the prisoner free ;
> His blood can make the foulest clean,
>   His blood availed for me.

CHAPTER X

JESUS AND ENTHUSIASM

Is Religious Enthusiasm Foolish?

During my college days I was on one occasion being entertained by a good fellow who unfortunately had not developed the social instinct. He showed me into his drawing room and we sat down.

'Beautiful day!' I remarked by way of opening a conversation.

'Yes,' replied my host. 'It is.'

'Quite nice for the holiday makers,' I continued.

'Yes, quite,' he replied, and then lapsed into silence.

'Have you had your holidays yet?' I asked.

'No, not yet,' he said.

Then there was a long pause in which I racked my brain for some topic of conversation calculated to interest this unsociable host.

'I see you have some nice pictures, are you interested in art?' I inquired.

'No—they are my sons,' was the answer.

That was no good. Looking round the room I espied a good piano, and commenting on the same I asked my friend if he played.

'No—it's my daughter who plays,' he explained.

I had failed again! Looking out of the window I noticed a well-kept bit of garden, and hoping my host would show an interest in horticulture, I asked him if he were interested in gardening.

' No—my wife looks after the garden,' he said. That had failed.

' Do you play golf ? ' I ventured after a little while. But he wasn't interested in golf.

Again there was a long silence ; and then in desperation I asked him if he had any hobby. But no, the unfortunate fellow hadn't even a hobby : and so I closed my eyes and had a nap until dinner was served.

On another occasion I was being entertained by a man who happened to be a golf enthusiast. We started to talk golf as soon as we met, and we talked golf the whole time. Again and again I tried to switch off the conversation to some other topic—but in vain, for he immediately brought me back to the old theme. He was golf mad ! He *was* enthusiastic—too much so !

Now the first man was really most unnatural. Man is naturally addicted to ruling passions ; to ' going crazy ' over things, as we say. Animals don't do it— but men do. Cows don't go crazy about chewing their cud, cats don't go crazy about catching mice, monkeys don't go crazy about cracking nuts, but there is hardly a thing from whippets to worship, from gambling to God, about which men do not tend to go crazy. We all of us do it. You say a thing is ' All the craze.' Women go crazy about short hair and short skirts. Men go crazy about long hair and skirt-like trousers. Most of us go crazy over football and cricket. Some of us go crazy over tennis. And so on.

And we call this peculiar human propensity ' enthusiasm.' The word ' enthusiasm ' is really a religious word and implies that men are possessed by a god. We sometimes say 'he makes a real religion of it'—and that is exactly what enthusiasm means —making a thing your god.

And this going crazy over things, this making a thing your god, this enthusiasm, is as I say, quite natural. The trouble with our modern world is that most folks go crazy over the wrong things. I have heard men who were enthusiastic almost to idiocy over some foolish pursuit like dog racing, laugh at other people's religious enthusiasms. Men consider it quite sane to go crazy over golf, cinema shows, football, Oxford bags, pigeons, whippets, tennis, test matches and tiddly-winks—but they consider it foolish or insane to go crazy over God.

But in reality the sanest thing you can do is to go crazy about God. Because if you are enthusiastic about Him, then naturally, your other enthusiasms will be controlled and directed by this supreme enthusiasm. The unfortunate thing is that most folks are crazy about themselves—the god they are possessed by is the god of self—they are selfish, self-centred.

But, someone may ask what does it matter whether a man is crazy about himself or about God ? It makes no difference. In other words, it doesn't matter what you believe. Doesn't it ? It's the only thing in all the world that does matter ! On it depends your worth as a citizen, and your worth as an immortal soul. To say that it does not matter, is to say that so long as you centre your whole life around someone or something, it doesn't matter in the least what it is. That's like saying you might as well worship a gorilla as worship God. It is the same as saying that the miser is as good as the devoted minister, that the bloated bookie is as good as the bishop, that the thief is as good as the teacher, that the vulgar honours hunter is as good as the healer of men. Which is manifestly absurd. Your belief is a vital thing, and it is a dangerous thing—it can blow you to heaven or blast you to hell.

If you are a ' Self-enthusiast ' you will seek to satisfy the desires and lusts of self—and that may end you in gaol, a madhouse, or the grave very quickly. When people are crazy about themselves, when they are self-centred, then other folks have to suffer. The self-enthusiast is greedy—and when men are greedy others have to go without things. A greedy man will gamble in the hope of getting something for nothing—and then if he loses, his wife and children will have to suffer ; and if he wins, some other wives and children suffer. A selfish Statesman may covet another nation's land—and so other innocent souls may be compelled to fight in wars, and women may have to suffer privations and loss of husband and son. When men are selfish they want cheap labour, and thus have slaves and underpaid workmen. When men are selfish they cry out for a maximum amount of pay with a minimum amount of work—and thus you get slackers. When men are selfish they seek to satisfy their personal desires without caring two hoots about others—thus you get prostitutes and other social wreckage. And so one could go on, tracing all the world's wrongs to enthusiasm for self. Self-centredness is the curse of the world.

And I really believe that it is only Christ enthusiasm —Christ craziness—that will save the world. If you are an enthusiast for God—if you are crazy about Christ

—then in your craziness you are reaching out to the highest form of sanity. Your passion for Him—if pure and strong—will control all your lesser enthusiasms. Through that passion your other passions will be elevated. Your interests will be directed from the low to the high, from the bad to the good, the beautiful, and the true. Instead of living for self-gratification, you will live for the good of others. You will love the Lord God with all your strength, and your neighbour as yourself. You will cease to be concerned about your health, stomach or pocket, and you will busy yourself with the serving of other people, with the relief of distress, the alleviation of suffering, the cheering of the sad, the strengthening of the weak, and so on. You will cease to be a nuisance to your neighbours, and become a blessing; you will cease to be a nonentity in your town, and become a power for good; you will cease to be a mere human unit, and will become a valuable citizen. The one and only way of saving the world is by making it Christ crazy.

Now let us turn from the individual to the Church. I think that one of the weaknesses of the Church of Christ to-day is a lack of enthusiasm. We are lukewarm. We are not stone cold, but we are not boiling hot. We are not indifferent, but we are not zealous. We lack enthusiasm—we need to go crazy about things.

In the second chapter of Revelation it says: ' I know thy works, and thy toil and thy patience, nevertheless I have somewhat against thee, because thou hast left thy first love.' The Church of Ephesus abounded in good works, and the writer appreciates the fact, I know thy works and thy toil and thy patience he says, but there was something lacking—what was

it ? It had fallen away from its first enthusiasm—
from its first love. The Church at Ephesus was
something like a young married couple. It had
enjoyed the wonderful, rapturous, romantic days of
courtship, and the ecstatic bliss of honeymoon and
early marriage. But familiarity was beginning to tell.
All married people know how it happens—the novelty
and excitement gone, they have to settle down to the
grim monotony of it all—washing pots, making beds,
scrubbing floors, cooking meals, paying bills, dodging the
tax collector and the gas man, trying to make endsmeet,
trying to please a bad-tempered husband—it knocks the
bottom out of the silver casket of romance, doesn't it ?
The feverish joy of the first love is gone, and, unless
you are a Pola Negri or a Charlie Chaplin, you've to
settle down to the humdrum monotony of it all !

That's the meaning of the metaphor ! The Church
at Ephesus had lost its first love. The eagerness of
its first conversion had gone out of it. It had settled
down to the ways of an established Church, with plenty
of good works and plenty of good people, but with a
loss of that first, spontaneous, passionate loyalty.
And unless it recruited its enthusiasm, said the
writer, it would cease to be.

How applicable that is to many Churches to-day !
They are energetic Churches, but they cannot truth-
fully be called enthusiastic Churches ! They have
their good people and their good works, and they have
their fruits—but they lack the enthusiasm of their
first love. There are lots of Churches to-day which
need shaking up, startling, awakening—they need
flooding with a new enthusiasm, permeating with a
pulsing passion. A blacksmith can do nothing with

the fire out, and a Church can do nothing without the burning heat of a passionate enthusiasm.

An enthusiast can do almost anything. If you tried to run a cricket club, as some folk try to run churches, it would be defunct before the end of the season. But start with enthusiasm—go crazy over the job—and it will be a rattling success. So it is with the Church. If we could regain the enthusiasm of the early days of Methodism our Churches would not be half empty but crammed full. If we would talk our Churches up instead of running them down, if we would work for them, and pray for them, and go to them as we did in our early conversion days—our churches would be filled in a very short time.

The trouble lies with us as individuals. We are perfectly respectable and entirely respected, but we've outgrown our enthusiasm. We've become unemotional and self-repressed. It's thought *infra dig* to get keen about religion. Let's go crazy for Christ. Let's do something impulsive, something impetuous or even foolish. Let's get intoxicated with Holy Zeal ! Our lives move like the River Rhine, which has its boisterous Alpine youth, and then runs more and more slowly, until in Holland you can hardly see whether it has any current or not. We start our Christian life with a youthful leap of enthusiasm, then we calm down and gradually lapse into cold stolidness.

Our religion needs more fire, more burning zeal. As the flames of a fire leap from one object to another consuming everything before them, so would a Church ablaze with zeal leap from one victory to another. On a Wayside Pulpit I once saw the words : ' Nothing great was ever achieved without enthusiasm '—and it's true.   'Nothing great was ever achieved without enthusiasm.'   Enthusiasm spells success.

> Be earnest, earnest—mad if thou wilt,
> Do what thou doest as if the stake were heaven,
> And this thy last deed ere the judgement day.
> When all's done, nothing's done.   Below let work be death,
> If work be love.

I wonder if you are taking me seriously ?   When I am preaching I wonder if the members of the congregation are listening, or merely pretending to listen, and really thinking what a funny hat Mrs. Jinks is wearing !

I was thinking about this the other night.   I went to a service and listened to another parson preach. It was a queer experience.   And I tried to get into the minds of the people sitting around me—what did it all mean to them ?   What were they thinking ?   Did they take it seriously ?   Very few did any singing worth calling singing—their lips moved, but although I listened hard I couldn't hear much—just one or two bold birds piping away lustily !   And the sermon ! Most of them sat perfectly still all through the sermon —you could have heard a pin drop !   But I wondered were they listening, or were they just polite !   It's a funny thing, this preaching business !   A man told me the other day that I preach too long !   Evidently he was bored.   I wonder if you are bored with this book ?   I hope not !

An old experienced speaker was giving advice to a young one who was about to make a maiden speech. And he said—' If you don't strike oil in the first few minutes, stop boring ! '   When that fellow told me I preach too long he set me thinking.   I wondered what he came to church for.   He even told me what he thought I ought to have said. But I couldn't have said what he suggested, because I didn't believe it. They were nice comfortable commonplaces, that he suggested. But I'm not going to say nice things I don't believe just to please people—I'd be a contemptible sneak if I did that, and every decent young man would despise me. But there are many people who don't want to hear one's honest attempt to get at truth—they don't want enlightening—they just want stroking till they purr like well-fed cats. And they've about as much intelligence as cats, some of 'em ! They're too well fed and comfortable !

There is a humorous story of a parson who was walking home with a farm labourer who was a regular attender at his church.

' Sunday must be a blessed day for you ! ' observed the parson.

' Aye, Sir,' replied the labourer, ' it is, indeed, a blessed day. I works hard all the week through, and then I comes to church o' Sundays, and sits me down, and lays me legs up, and thinks o' nothin' ! '

I'm afraid the farm labourer isn't the only one who thinks of nothin' in church.

I remember how during my early apprenticeship days I didn't take preachers particularly seriously. There weren't many of us apprentices went to church, but those of us who did, went more because we liked the girls in the choir than to hear a sermon. As a matter of fact, we looked at snap shots and the contents of our wallets during the sermon—we didn't take the parson seriously at all. We took our work seriously, and like true Britishers took our pleasure seriously too—but parsons and sermons, No ! To be perfectly honest, we thought parsons queer old birds with their feet trampling down the clay of cemeteries, and their heads stuck among the clouds listening for the harps of heaven, and we made uncomplimentary sketches of them, in their round hats, and long coats, and bulky umbrellas, in chalk on the castings in the workshops.

But all that's changed now. I can see now that it was our ignorance which was to blame. People usually scoff at things they don't understand. I thought religion was just an affair of churches and creeds and curates ! I never thought of it as vital.

Then someone took my attention from churches and parsons to Christ. I started to read my New Testament—and all the other books on Christ I could get hold of. And the more I read the more enthralled I became, and the more enthralled the more enthusiastic. I went crazy about Christ. I saw Him to be, not the effeminate, stained-glass figure I'd imagined Him to be, but a virile robust young man—the cleanest, bravest, most splendid fellow I'd ever heard of, or read of ! And slowly it dawned upon me that if every one lived like Him, this old earth would be a topping place to live in—in fact, that was the most top hole and splendid thing I could think of—a world full of Christs or Christ-like people. And I saw that if His teaching were practised as well as preached— goodness gracious—what a revolution there'd be ! Strikes, and slaves, and slums, and lockouts, and wars, and the white slave traffic, and all the rotten mire and filth of our civilization would vanish, as mists vanish before the rising sun.

And so I gave up my job to devote my life to getting folk to see as I see—to get them to live the Christ way.

9

That's why I'm a parson ; and that's why I preach long sermons—I've so much to say and so little time to say it in—I'm just overflowing with love and devotion to Christ that I want others to feel as I feel—I want others to go crazy about Christ.

I wonder if you've ever thought much about it ? I don't want you to go crazy about Churches and creeds and conferences and all those other things we've emphasized so much in the past. It's Christ I want you to be keen about—the Christ of Galilee— the Christ of Calvary : the One who was spat on and nailed to a cross, but who somehow or other still lives and dominates the thoughts of men.

Even a cynic like Bernard Shaw has to admit that the Christ-ideal is the best he knows. He says : ' We have always had a curious feeling that though we crucified Christ on a stick, He somehow managed to get the right end of it, and that if we were better men we might try His plan.'

A Hindu once said : ' The problems of the day arise through the lack of the spirit of Jesus Christ in the affairs of men.'

I believe that. Let those of us who call ourselves by His name, try to get the Christ-Spirit in our own hearts and our own affairs.

Let me, in closing, paint you a picture. It is night time. Overhead a great purple sky hangs serenely dotted with a million silvery stars. We are looking down upon the streets of a city. The shop windows and street lamps flood the pavement with light. Trams, buses, motor-cars, rush along the roads. The pavements are thronged with gaily-dressed human beings—and they are all busy, scurrying about like ants in a disturbed nest. Golfers come slouching from the station gates, with their clubs slung over their shoulders, after the day's hard play. Football enthusiasts sing and shout as their charabancs drive through the busy streets. Shopkeepers hurry and scurry to please their late customers. Uniformed men stand at the glittering doors of theatres and picture shows inviting patrons, and suggesting that all seats are guaranteed. Painted women, like butterflies, flit from cars to cabarets, men in their black and white evening suits move like animated tailors' dummies— (you know the sort of thing—a typical Saturday evening crowd—every one going crazy over his or her own particular pursuit).

And then, in the night sky, very faint above the glare of the lights, I see a quiet figure. It is not a Western figure—it is an Eastern, clad in oriental robes, with a well-chisled face and a pointed beard. And He appears to be sitting on a remote mountain rock, looking down through the mists upon the city streets. And as I watch Him I think I see tears in His eyes ; and I hear a soft voice—something like a mother's crooning to her sleeping child—and the voice is saying : ' Thou that stonest them that are sent unto thee, how oft would I have gathered thy children together, even as a hen gathereth her chickens under her wing, and ye would not ! '

But the crowd goes by unheeding. And when next I look for that Eastern figure, I see instead, a gleam of red in the night sky—a furnace door has been opened and has thrown its warm glow into the darkness ; and, standing out boldly against that blood-red sky I see—jet black—a wooden cross. And a voice says : ' Father, forgive them—they know not what they do.'

CHAPTER XI

JESUS AND TRAGEDY

Can Triumph Come Through Tragedy ?

It is nearly dark. Before us there stretches a vast expanse of grey undulating country, with here and there, like a pale ghost, a white-walled house. The last rays of the sunset are fading, and a long thin stretch of crimson sky shows—like a stream of blood—between a rift in the dark clouds. Against this slender finger of sunset light there stands out in bold relief the silhouette of a rounded hill, with on its summit—grim and black—three wooden crosses. . . . They are empty!

On two of these gibbets criminals have suffered the torture Rome considered fitting for their crimes. They, apart for their connexion with the third, are forgotten. But on the other there has suffered One whose name is now known as ' The Name above every name,' and who has made His influence felt throughout 1900 years of history. And that cross on which He suffered such a painful death (instrument of torture though it be) has become the symbol of all we hold noble and good, and has stirred the imaginations, touched the hearts, and moved the minds of men, as nothing else has ever done.

And, curious to relate, no matter how men may try,

they cannot escape that Cross! As it loomed there above the hills and valleys of Palestine 1900 years ago, so ever since, it has loomed above the undulations of History; and with a strange persistence the influence of its victim still endures. The thought of Him haunts the minds of men with the unsolved problem of the secret of His power, His spirit comes vibrant and alive from those eastern hills, and His challenges disturb our peace of mind.

As Jesus of Nazareth hung there on the Cross of Calvary, over 1900 years ago, it seemed as though He was defeated; but, as we look back now, we can see that, by a strange paradox, He has been Victorious. And it is of the victory that came through that apparent defeat that I wish to write in this chapter.

Let me first of all try, however inadequately, to stage for you the drama which was enacted around that Cross. The stage is set with a lavish display of light and colour. It is midday, and April. The scene is laid in Jerusalem—that ancient city of David, whose gold Temple pinnacles glitter in the sunshine. To-day is 'The Day of Preparation,' for to-morrow there is to be observed the greatest of Jewish festivals—'The Passover.' In every house a lamb will be slaughtered and its blood sprinkled on the house door. In the Temple, lambs will be slain, their blood sprinkled before the altar by the priests, and the fat offered—amid the chanting of psalms—as burnt sacrifices. In every home young lambs will be roasted and eaten, along with unleaven cakes and bitter herbs, and rich red wine drunk. The posture of the meal will be recumbent (a token of the rest God has given his people). There will be much saying of ' grace,' washing of hands, and offering of prayers. And then, with the second cup of wine, the son of each household will ask a question as to the meaning of the feast, and the father recite an explanation.

On the flat roofs of the houses the fleeces of lambs can be seen stretched out in the sun to dry, and from every house a thread of smoke curls upwards. Old hags with crooked noses come forth from the alleys, mumbling curses; dirty children hop along with bundles under their arms; bearded men hurry by, bearing a kid or a cask of wine upon their shoulders; donkey drivers pass, dragging stubborn donkeys by the halter. In every house the wife is preparing all that will be necessary for the feast, because for twenty-four hours no work is to be done. The streets and the houses resound with the hum of industry. Every one is busy.

But to-day there is a grim irony about all this preparation, for there passes through the narrow streets as grim and sinister a procession as ever was witnessed —it is a procession of death. While many in the city are preparing to offer to God their burnt sacrifices, others are preparing to sacrifice, in another way, God's most precious gift. Everywhere is joy and happiness, and through it all there walk three condemned criminals, each carrying the cross on which he is to suffer and die. While the city sings its praises to God, and men stretch themselves upon their couches around the festive board, drinking their symbolic wine, these three men must stretch upon their crosses and drink the wine of bitterness, and when their bodies are stiff with death they will be buried in the cold earth.

A mounted centurion, splendid in his uniform, shining armour, purple cloak and plumed helmet, rides at the head of the procession, and, as his prancing charger strains at the bit and tosses its head with annoyance at being compelled to walk with such solemn dignity, the crowd falls back and gazes at the three victims who are sweating beneath their awesome burdens. One of the victims is strong and defiant; another looks cunningly and maliciously at the onlookers; while the third—pale and worn—falters at every step.

The crosses are not heavy, for the Romans never waste wood upon their victims. But the exhaustion of Jesus is not to be wondered at, for during the last twenty-four hours He has been through a series of ordeals which would have tried the strength of any man. Last night He passed through such a mental and spiritual struggle that His sweat was even as blood. Then there had come the heartache of being betrayed by a friend, then the arrest followed by a night of horror when, tossed about like a shuttlecock, He had suffered the indignity of illegal examinations before a high priest, a subject-king, and a Roman procurator. There had been the weary journeyings from judge to judge, the cruelty of the heartless soldiers, the insults, the blows, the flogging! Then they had covered His bleeding and perspiring body with a purple horse-cloth, and, pretending Him to be a king, mockingly placed a crown of thorns upon His head.

Little wonder that He now appears no longer as that vigorous young man who, only a few days ago, took a whip, and cleared the Temple's shameful market-place. His radiant face now is drawn with pain ; His eyes, strained with unshed tears, are dull and sunken ; His clothes stick to His lacerated shoulders, and His body aches with weariness.

Crowds are always interested in what is morbid, and the Jews are no exception. And in a very short time a large rabble is following the sinister procession to its destination.

Round the neck of each criminal is tied a label describing his crime, and members of the crowd strain their necks in an effort to read the inscriptions. Some Pharisees who follow in the wake of the procession hurl abuse at Jesus. A few women, their faces veiled according to custom, weep softly as they follow their loved One to His place of execution.

Suddenly the procession's doleful progress is arrested, for ' The Man of Sorrows ' has stumbled beneath His load, and fainted. His olive skin has become ghastly pale, and the inflamed lids have closed over His tired eyes. The centurion, impatiently wheeling his prancing horse, utters a curse. Some soldiers, uttering threats, rush to the prostrate figure. The crowd gapes.

' He's pretending ! ' someone yells.

' Lift Him up—flog Him ! ' cries another.

' He's a hypocrite,' cries a third, ' make Him bear the cross to the end—that's the law ! '

' He called Himself a king,' someone sneers : ' Look at Him now—a king sprawling in the dirt.'

The centurion is impatient—he wants to get the business over, and, being a man of experience, sees that Jesus will never be able to carry the cross as far as the Place of the Skull, and so looks about for someone who might relieve Him of the burden. Selecting

a robust stranger he cries : ' Carry the cross for Him ! '
To refuse to obey a Roman soldier is a crime punishable
by a flogging, and the man complies at once.   Jesus
is raised to His feet and the procession proceeds.

The place of execution is a round chalky knoll
resembling a skull in shape.   Close by, two main roads,
one from Jaffa and one from Damascus, intersect.
And, as there are always many passing pilgrims and
traders, the Romans have selected this public place
as the scene of their executions, so that all beholding
the hanging victims may take warning.

From the city gate the road stretches like a long
white tape over an expanse of beautiful undulating
country—the yellow of the soil, the white chalk rocks,
the olive green of the grass, and the rich dark green
of the cyprus trees, mingling to make a patchwork of
fascinating beauty.   The sun's rays flood the scene with
quivering light, and the birds singing in the distant
orchards flood the air with liquid music.   This indeed
would be a lovely place in which to rest and dream.
But to-day is no day for dreams ; a discord spoils the
music's harmony—the discord of harsh human voices
chanting a dirge of death ; and the tranquillity of the
scene is disturbed by the appearance of that ghastly
procession as it emerges from the city gate.   Down the
long road it moves, with white dust hanging over it
like a cloud of ominous portent.   Then over the summit
of the skull-shaped hill the crowd swarms, as the
soldiers commence their cruel task.

Perhaps it would be kind if someone were to pass a
hand over our eyes, and so blot the rest of the scene
from our vision.   To say the least it is revolting, and
good taste will draw back in horror.   But it is not

always good to have our eyes blinded against grim reality. There is such a thing as a fool's paradise ! To understand human nature one must consider its sinners as well as its saints, one must look at its ugliness as well as its beauty, its horribleness as well as its' heroism. And if we are to understand Jesus, we must realize as fully as is possible the unspeakable cruelty, the unimaginable humiliation and the untold pain of His death.

The restless crowd is hushed into awesome silence as Jesus, divested of His garments, is nailed out on the cross as it lies on the ground. A legionary, hammer in hand, seizes one of the hands of Jesus—one of those hands which have healed lepers and caressed the heads of little children—and pushing it against the wood, poses the nail against the palm, and, with a quick sure blow, drives it through the flesh into the wood of the cross. A little blood spurting from the pierced palm stains the soldier's hand. In a similar way the other hand and the feet are fastened to the cross. But no cry escaped the lips of Jesus. Then with a shout and a heave the cross is hoisted aloft and jolted into its socket. The wrench tears the flesh. The face of Jesus is drawn with agony, and one hot tear rushes down His cheek, and mingles with the blood which trickles from His thorny crown—He has held it back till now, but at last it seems as though His heart will break. Slowly the red blood drips down to stain the white chalk beneath ; and down the stem of the cross there flows a thin red line.

And the crowd stands watching. ' And the people stood beholding ! ' Luke says. Yes, the people stood beholding. But not *all* the people. The world is not entirely evil. We are not all utterly bad. There *is* goodness in the world and there *are* good people. And even in that crucifixion crowd there are those who still love Christ. The Pharisees mock Him, the roughs laugh at Him, the priests scorn Him, and the soldiers gamble with His garments. But in that crowd there are those who look at Him through their tears ; there are those who feel a mental pang with each stroke of the hammer, and whose hearts feel pierced as His hands are pierced. Jesus was not altogether deserted in His pain, and when the rest have gone and the sun begins to sink in the west there will be seen a little group of mourners weeping at the foot of the cross.

That Calvary crowd, I think, represents the world in miniature. There are those to-day who still cry : ' Away with Him.' Those who jeer and scoff, those who pierce His sacred hands. There are even priests who continue to ' crucify afresh the Son of God.' But there are still those who love Him—those who still shed silent tears over His agony, those who marvel at His courage, and who wonder at His love. There are still those who in spite of doubt and uncertainty can cry, as Studdert Kennedy did just before his death, that they are prepared to follow Christ ' to the last ditch.'

We are told that to-day people as a whole are in-different to religion. That may be true. But are they indifferent about Jesus ? I wonder ! . . . At any rate of this I am certain, the world cannot remain indifferent about Him. His personality has forced itself upon every age since His death, and it is forcing itself upon our age with more persistence than ever. And we've got to make up our minds about Him.

In one of his characteristic passages Mr. Studdert Kennedy once wrote :

'Through the vast complexities of our modern civilized world made one by God, the crucified Christ is looking down upon us—with death in His bleeding hands and feet—but life in the light of His burning eyes—and demanding from us all—every individual man and woman—a choice between the glory of Reason, Patience, and Love, and the glory of Force, and Wrath and Fear. . . . He will not go away. . . . He is making us waver all over the world. He is going to drive us to a decision with His wounded hands. He will not let us have the world for a playground, a battlefield, a factory, an empire any longer ; we must give it to Him. We must give it to Him or—or there will be darkness all over the earth from the sixth hour until the ninth—and that may be a thousand years. We must decide, and this decision is for you and me.'[1]

Studdert Kennedy was right. We must decide. We must decide as a nation and as individuals. If we do not, our nation will go the way of Rome and Babylon, and we shall find in our own private lives a hopelessness that cannot be cheered, a discord that cannot be harmonized, and a restlessness that cannot be quieted.

In his play 'The Terrible Meek,' Mr. Charles Rann Kennedy stages a conversation between the mother of Jesus and the centurion on guard as they stand at the foot of the cross when every one else has gone. The soldier is muttering to himself. Mary overhears his musings.

[1] *The Word and the Work*. p. 80, 84.

'I don't understand you,' she says. 'Only a little while ago I heard His blood dripping down here in the darkness. The stones are dank with it. Not an hour ago. He's dead.'

'He's alive,' says the centurion.

'Why do you mock me?' she asks. 'Are you God that you can kill and make alive, all in one breath?'

And the captain replies: 'He's alive. I can't kill Him. All the empires can't kill Him. How shall hate kill the power that possesses and rules the earth? . . . Listen . . . I am a soldier. I have been helping to build kingdoms for over twenty years. I have never known any other trade. Soldiery, bloodshed, murder: that's my business. My hands are crimson with it. That's what empire means. We stretch out our hands, greedy, grasping, tyrannical, to possess the earth. It can't last: it never has lasted, this building in blood and fear. Already our kingdoms begin to totter. Possess the earth! We have lost it. We never did possess it: for the soul of the earth is man and the love of him, and we have made of both a desolation.

'I tell you woman, this dead son of yours, disfigured, shamed, spat upon, has built a kingdom this day that can never die. The living glory of Him rules it. The earth is His and He made it. . . . Something has happened up here on this hill to-day to shake all the kingdoms of blood and fear to dust. . . . The meek, the terrible meek, the fierce agonizing meek, are about to enter into their inheritance.'[1]

How true that is we do not really realize. . . . 'We stretch out our hands, greedy, grasping, tyrannical,

[1] *The Terrible Meek*. Charles Rann Kennedy. 1912. p. 36–39.

to possess the earth. . . . It cannot last—it never has lasted, this building in blood and fear.' The Roman Empire, which was instrumental in destroying Jesus—once the mightiest empire in the world—has decayed. The kingdom of blood and fear has not lasted. So too with the Babylonian Empire, so too with the Egyptian. Kingdoms of blood and fear do not last. But the Kingdom of Love that Jesus set out to establish has lasted. Through apparent defeat He has achieved victory. Evil may seem to dominate for a time—but ultimately goodness triumphs.

Whether you believe in the physical resurrection of Jesus or not, you cannot deny His victory. From the Cross there has radiated an influence which has changed the world. There is hardly a phase of life that has not been touched by Jesus. And His power is increasing. The Church may be failing but not the Christ. It has been said that there is more real vital interest in Christ to-day than ever there was. Fifty years ago He was locked within the walls of our churches where He was worshipped on Sundays, and by many neglected for the rest of the week. He was spoken of with awe and timidity—His Name was one that could be uttered on Sundays when one was suitably clad, but not mentioned on the golf links or in the workshop. He was written of in a technical and ecclesiastical way, and read of by scholars and priests.

But now He is free. He has broken down the church doors which were His prison. Now He is out in the open street, the market and the shop. You can hear Him being discussed in railway trains and on the golf links, you can read of Him in a hundred popular and cheap books, you can find Him being

written of by eminent novelists and literary critics,
you can read of Him in almost any newspaper, you
can hear men's thoughts of Him expressed in plays
on the stage, you can see His life portrayed in at
least three films on the cinema screen. In scores of
world conferences men and women of almost every
nation have met to discuss Him. In universities
students gather during the evenings to talk of Him.
We are gradually realizing that we cannot leave Him
out of our Politics and Industry. His Kingdom is
growing. And His Cross, which was once an instrument of torture and a symbol of shame, has now
become the symbol of salvation, and it hangs as an
ornament from the neck of Beauty, it towers above
city streets, and blazes from the flags of armies and the
standards of navies. . . .Christ's missionaries are in
almost every land. *He has conquered !*

' I tell you . . . this dead son of yours has this day
built a kingdom that can never die.'

Mr. Walter Russell Bowie, pointing out how Jesus
at the beginning of His ministry, proclaimed another
Kingdom, says : ' Jesus was proclaiming another
Kingdom, which should be more important than the
empire Tiberius ruled. He proclaimed a power which
was yet invisible, as against the immensely visible and
ponderable power of Rome. And the curious, plain
fact of history is this : that not only has the empire
of Tiberius crumbled, but Tiberius himself has so
faded into the limbo of the dead that no single
individual on earth to-day has any flicker of personal
emotion concerning anything he thought or did ; while
Jesus of Nazareth, who seemed to have behind Him
less force than the least of the legionaries of Tiberius,

is linked with the most vital concerns of multitudes in every generation.' [1]

What is the explanation ? Why should there be all this interest in a man who lived 1900 years ago ? We do not usually take so much interest in the dead ! It is estimated that sixty billion people have lived upon this earth since the dawn of history. Of these most are forgotten. A few have been remembered a few years. How many names have lasted for two thousand years ? A few hundreds only—against the myriads of forgotten.

And those are remembered because of some great achievement—Alexander the Great because the world shook at the tread of his armies. Aristotle and Plato because they put into written words the philosophies which had been handed down through the ages. The Pharaohs because they built the mighty pyramids. And so on. But none of these things is true of Jesus. He did not command armies, He did not write philosophies, He did not erect monuments. How is it that He still persists ? It is because there was that about Jesus which is to be found in no other. There is about Him something super human. And so we say that He was ' divine.' He was indeed the Son of God. And He still lives.

Giovanni Papini—the converted Italian—writes : ' Caesar was more talked about in his time than Jesus, and Plato taught more science than Christ. People still discuss the Roman ruler and the Greek philosopher, but who nowadays is hotly for Caesar or against him ; and where now are the Platonists and anti-Platonists ? Christ, on the contrary, is still living among us. There

1 *The Master.* p. 110.

are still people who love Him and who hate Him. There is a passion for the love of Christ, and a passion for His destruction. The fury of so many against Him is proof that He is not dead.' [1]

Papini cannot be classed as a logician. But one has to admit that the mere fact that I am writing of Him, or you reading of Him, is evidence that Jesus is unique. He was no writer, He was no orator—He just taught a handful of unpromising men for three years—and then was done to death. And yet He still persists. It baffles our understanding—and so we can only say ' He is risen.'

Yes, He is risen—and our belief in His resurrection has a historical basis ; the existence of the Church is its proof. If Christ's dead body had remained in the tomb, Christianity would never have spread, Paul would never have been converted, and the Lord's Day would never have existed.

There are those in every church throughout the world who can testify to a consciousness in their hearts and lives of the presence of the spirit of that same Jesus.

Here are three classic testimonies : Along the desolate shores of Labrador—one of the coldest places on earth—among the missions and hospitals he has founded, lives Sir Wilfred Grenfell. Writing of *What Christ Means to Me*, he says : ' The faith in Christ upon which I have based my life has given me a light on life's meaning which has satisfied my mind, body and soul. Faith came to me with the vision of Christ still alive in the world to-day. He meant to me a determination, God helping me, to follow Him.'

[1] *The Story of Christ.*

Out there in the heat and loneliness of Equatorial Africa—one of the hottest places in the world—lives Dr. Albert Schweitzer—doctor of medicine, doctor of music, doctor of theology ; philosopher, physician, writer and missionary—of whom says one writer : ' There has never been a more striking case of a man having " left all " to follow his ideal of service to needy humanity.' What is the motive power behind that colossal sacrifice ? It is the same Jesus. Listen to Dr. Schweitzer, as in his book, *On the Edge of the Primaeval Forest*, he describes the close of an operation : ' The operation is finished, and in the hardly-lighted dormitory I watch for the sick man's awakening. Scarcely has he recovered consciousness when he stares about him and ejaculates again and again : " I've no more pain ! I've no more pain ! " . . . His hand feels for mine and will not let it go. Then I begin to tell him and the others who are in the room that it is the Lord Jesus who has told the doctor and his wife to come and care for the sick negroes.'

Out in India—one of the most fascinating countries in the world—working among the aristocrats and intellectualists of that great peninsula is Dr. Stanley Jones—once a lawyer, now a missionary. Once he tells us he thought he had to be God's lawyer making magnificent defences in His Name, but now he is to be God's witness telling of what God has done for Him. And he tells us that the dynamic of his life is simply Jesus. ' I asked an earnest Hindu one day what he thought of Christ,' says Mr. Jones in *The Christ of the Indian Road*. ' He thoughtfully answered : " There is no one else who is seriously bidding for the heart of the world except Jesus Christ. There is no one else on the field." And Mr. Jones comments : ' Sweep the horizon—is there any one else ? '

I know of no one.

' Whom else,' asks the American writer, Bowie, in *The Master*, ' Whom else is there to follow on the road that leads to more abundant life ? '

To that question there is but one answer—there is Jesus only !

The Rev. Silvester Horne once truly said : ' The only thing that really matters is that we give ourselves to Christ, to live, to work, think and dare for Him. That is everything.' It is everything.

CHAPTER XII

JESUS AND SUNDAY

WHY KEEP SUNDAY?

THIS is an age which refuses to accept anything as a matter of course. Our grandfathers and great grandfathers before us were apt to accept whatever ' was ' without much question. If an institution or a custom existed, the mere fact that it *did* exist justified its existence, and the fact that it was English made it either perfect or as near perfect as anything in this world can be.

But that attitude has gone, and in its place we moderns have put one of daring and ruthless criticism. Refusing to take anything for granted to-day, we want to know the ' reason why.' Conventional assumptions do not satisfy—we suspect that many venerable institutions have outlived their usefulness.

One of the institutions which our forefathers accepted without question was the Christian Sunday, a day when all respectable people went to church largely as a matter of public duty. According to some, the Victorian and Edwardian sabbaths were as stiff and uncomfortable as the new clothes which were so essential. It was a matter of morning service followed by church parade—when gentlemen, splendid in top hats and long coats, walked in dignified manner beside sedate ladies, dressed up like characters in comic opera in little hats, mountainous hair, and crinolines, or leg-of-mutton sleeves, wasp waists, bustles and voluminous skirts. Then there was the dreary afternoon when there was nothing to do but read sacred literature, walk sedately, or sit in the park, or go to sleep. Then evening service again, family prayers, and so to bed. It was a day of quiet streets, and closed shops, when the still air was disturbed only by the music of church bells. For children it was a day to be dreaded—a day of clean frocks—and strict discipline ; a day when one might read nothing secular, play with no toys, sing nothing but sacred music, and do nothing but what was considered ' proper.'

(Let me hasten to add, as one whose childhood was spent in Edwardian days, that Sunday was never a dreary day in our home.)

Then came the War, violently upsetting the ordered life of the nation, so that men who had spent their Sunday mornings in church found themselves spending them coaling ships or acting as camp scavengers ; boys who had spent the Sunday afternoon in Sunday School singing ' Gentle Jesus Meek and Mild ' found themselves throwing bombs at Germans and singing ' O my, I don't want to die, I want to go home.' Very often they would spend days on end in wet, cold trenches until Sunday went past unnoticed.

And so, almost unconsciously, the old-time Sunday slipped quietly away. When peace came men found it difficult to settle down to normal conditions. After spending years in a man-made hell, it was a little difficult to sit in a church and sing about heaven ; after hurling lead and bombs and things at other

fellows' heads for so long, they found it difficult to
start thinking about 'love' and 'brotherhood' and
such like sentiment.   After spending every day in
scientific and wholesale murder, they found it a
little inconsistent to recite such commands as 'Thou
shalt not kill.'   And so many of them spent the
Sundays at home as they had spent them in the Army
—just like any other day ; so it was that eventually
Sunday games, shops, cinemas, &c., became the usual
instead of the unusual thing.   And to-day the first
day of the week in seaside resorts like Scarborough
and Blackpool is almost like any other day.

But the modern Sunday has not come without a
certain amount of indignant protest.   There are still
a few who think that Sunday should be different from
other days.   Men of influence feel so strongly on the
subject that they are prepared to make a bold protest,
as Sir Arthur Atkinson did in Hull when he resigned
from the Aero Club in the summer of 1931 as a protest
against the Air Pageant which had been arranged for
a Sunday.   And the fact that in Manchester, where a
similar Pageant was arranged to be held on a Sunday,
public feeling was so strong that the date had to be
changed in less than a week, shows that the British
Nonconformist Conscience is not yet dead !

Now, what about it ?   Isn't it a lot of fuss over
nothing ?   The continental Sunday is now almost an
established thing—why make all the to-do about it ?
Why not let the Pagans have the Pageants, and the
Christians the Churches ?   Surely they are free agents
—Why can't they be left to please themselves ?

Well, a fool can ask a question, but it often takes
a wise person to answer it.   Of course it is quite easy

to be piously dogmatic and to say that Sunday is the Lord's Day and therefore must be kept sacred, and that if we don't keep it sacred we must expect the punishment that always follows unrighteousness.

But intelligent people won't listen to that sort of thing—they call it ' tripe ' and ' bunkum.' If the Christian Sunday is to be kept as a day different from any other day, then people want to know why. Why shouldn't we play games on Sundays—if not, why not ?

It must be admitted that the question is a difficult one, and each person must think the matter out carefully for himself. Perhaps the following suggestions may be helpful.

First : *Why have a Sunday at all ?* Why not a seven day week, and leave the religious folk to arrange their meetings as they like. Why set one day aside as different from all the others ?

1. Because man's physical nature demands rest and change. You can flog the human will so that every day of the week is a day of equal mental and physical effort, but you cannot go on like that indefinitely. There comes a breaking point.

As Lord Macaulay once truly said : ' We are not poorer, but richer, because we have through many ages rested from our labour one day in seven. That day is not lost. While industry is suspended, while the plough lies in the furrow, while the Exchange is silent, while no smoke ascends from the factory, a process is going on quite as important to the wealth of the nation as any process which is performed on more busy days. Man, the machine of machines . . . is repairing and winding up, so that he returns to his labours on the Monday with clearer intellect, livelier spirits, with renewed corporal vigour.'

It is significant that the Parliamentary Committee on the Sunday closing of shops in 1905 received resolutions and petitions in favour of Sunday closing from 300 shopkeepers' associations, 490 Urban District Councils, the corporations of many boroughs and towns, and 160 Trade Unions. And the Committee reported that an overwhelming number of tradesmen were in favour of Sunday closing. No sane person wants a seven day working week. The body demands one rest day.

That is a point I hardly need enlarge—it is so evident —any doctor or psychologist will support me. And it was to satisfy the need of periodical rest that the sacred days of Babylon were observed in the far off days of our civilization.

Then in Israel, in the long, long ago, when Moses was leading his wandering tribes about the wastes of the East, there was enforced the law which said : ' Six days shalt thou labour and do thy work, and on the Seventh day thou shalt rest, that thine ox and thine ass may have rest, and the son of thy handmaid, and the stranger may be refreshed ' (Ex. XXIII. 12). This sacred day of rest was observed all through the troubled history of Israel. It was a day of joy and delight, for we read : ' Go your way, eat the fat and drink the sweet, and send portions unto him for whom nothing is prepared, for the day is holy unto the Lord ; neither be ye grieved, for the joy of the Lord is your strength.'

But by the time of Christ the professional preachers of the day had so hedged the Sabbath with silly regulations and restrictions that He had on several occasions to sting their pasty piety by his sharp retorts, which some would suppose have a relaxing tendency.

But if you will study His teaching on the Sabbath question carefully, you'll find that His road does not lead to a secularized day, and to the abandoning of reasonable religious duties, but to a conscientious care of the day and its best customs, in the twin interests of religion and rest. Jesus was at war with humbug; and He upset the Pharisees' applecarts because they paid more attention to Sabbath regulations than to what the Sabbath stood for. Jesus wasn't such a revolutionist as some would suppose. We must not forget that He was a loyal member of the Synagogue, dedicated at birth, and very frequently found complying with good customs. He travelled to the feasts, frequented the Temple and was deeply concerned for its honour. He approved of Tribute and paid the Temple tax. And you will remember Luke plainly states, 'He came to Nazareth where He had been brought up, and he entered, as was His custom, into the Synagogue on the Sabbath Day.'

In the first century Christianity, beginning at Jerusalem, spread in all directions. Soon there came a break with Judaism. There were foreign Christians as well as Jewish, and the foreigners had not been accustomed to observe Jewish laws or to keep holy the Seventh Day. And as the years passed, increasing reflections upon Christian teaching seemed to show, that in changing the passover into the Supper of Remembrance, and by setting Himself as the Bread of Life in place of the Manna, and a score of other things He had done and said, Jesus had in mind something larger than Judaism. And so, gradually Jewish laws and customs began to lose their grip, and eventually the old Jewish Sabbath began to lose its claim. And a new day began to take the first place in their regard. That was the *first* day of the week. It was on the first day of the week that the Master had risen from the dead, and had also appeared to them five times. And these wonderful memories turned into *Expectations* and made them associate the first day and not the Seventh with His advent. And so the First day became ' Our Lord's Day ' and became the customary day for them to assemble.

And so with the gradual evolution of the organization we call Christianity, the Church took up, I think, a better day than it laid down ; the old was a backward looking day and ended the week ; the new a forward looking day and began the week afresh. The old day had been steeped in the spirit of rest ; but the new had the atmosphere of fresh life and creative action. The old day had stood for tradition, the new stood for pioneering—progress : it was a day associated in their minds with such commands as ' go ' and ' make '— ' go into all the world and make disciples of all nations.' It stood for new hope, new life, new enterprise—it was the day of salvation, the day when spiritual strength was renewed and enthusiasm rekindled.

And so as the ages rolled by *the day* remained as the Lord's Day, and it became to many, not as some would suppose, a day of oppression, but a day of opportunity.

And that is why some of us are so anxious to preserve the sacredness of Sunday, we haven't forgotten its significance. To us it is *the day*. It is to us the symbol of that redemptive force which has been as a fly wheel on our British civilization—a force which has kept us stable, given to us most of our best qualities and institutions, and saved us on several occasions from running headlong into disaster. Just as Armistice Day has become with us a Day of Remembrance, so the Christian Sunday soon became in Britain the day set apart for the national recognition of Christianity as our national religion. It was an outward visible sign to the whole world that we Britishers were a nation with a sense of reverence deep down in our hearts, an admiration for real nobility, and an appreciation of Christian idealism. Sunday was the badge that showed to the world that we were trying, perhaps unsuccessfully, but nevertheless sincerely, to live up to that lofty standard of Manhood set by Christ.

And I am terribly afraid that our present desire to discard the badge is a sign that we have lost the sense of reverence, the admiration of real nobility, and the appreciation of Christian idealism for which Sunday has stood so long.

And so it resolves itself into this—the Sunday controversy is really a conflict between two ideals of life. The Christian Sunday stands for a conception of life as spiritual and not simply physical. It symbolizes the belief that there are things more important than gain or pleasure. The people who are crying out for a brighter Sunday, and shouting ' Why can't we do as we like,' are (perhaps unconsciously) advocating undiluted selfishness—it's do as we like— not as the nation as a whole likes—every man to please himself.

Sunday symbolizes the belief that life misses its mark when it seeks simply self-gratification. If these silly people who talk so loudly and glibly about 'freedom' and 'liberty' would stop to think awhile before they speak, they would realize that liberty does not mean licence ; that real liberty is based upon limitation. If the piston of an engine is to be effective it must be left free ; but its freedom consists not in isolation but in perfect adjustment to all parts of the machine. It is free not when isolated and left alone, but when skilfully and carefully associated with other parts of the great structure. So with human life. No man is free in the sense that he can live irrespective of his fellows. We are all limited. And it is a curious paradox of life that in the moral sphere the greater the limitation the greater the power. That's the meaning of Christ's words ' let him deny himself '—' let him limit himself.'

That argument of let ' me please myself ' doesn't do. It is because people will persist in pleasing themselves that we have to maintain such institutes as police forces, prisons and asylums. Perhaps if some of these ' liberty ' people would take Christianity a little more seriously, and give it as much thought as they give their business and pleasure, there would not be such need for police forces, prisons and asylums.

We mustn't forget that it is Christianity which has made our British race what it is. It is Christianity which has made life to-day as tolerable and comfortable as it is. Your hospitals, your schools, your universities, your cottage homes, your cheap press, your respect for motherhood, your reverence for childhood, the very liberty about which so many crow, are due, all of them, to the influence of this thing we call Christianity. And Christianity owes its place in our national life to a great extent to the fact that the first day of the week had been preserved as Christ's Day, a day exclusive for worship and instruction in Christian idealism.

When the enthusiastic golfer awakes on a Sunday morning and thinks of a little white ball lying on a vivid green fairway, and recalls the joy he has had other Sunday mornings hitting that little white ball with all his might and skill, he should stop to think too of other and more important things than little white balls on green grass. He should think of the part that religion is playing in life, the crises into which it is continuously coming, the influence it has had on the past, the toil and sacrifice by which it has been handed on, the swaying battle with the world's selfishness, the human blood that has been shed at the stake to preserve it ; he should remember that maybe some of his own forefathers suffered persecution and pain for the sake of it ; and remembering this, he should realize that this tremendous moral force, this force which fights for truth, honesty and idealism, needs every decent man's aid. He should realize the need for concentrated action so that the best things in it may be provided for and made to prevail.

If he is a man at all he will, under the influence of these larger views, gladly choose another day for his game, rather than help, by his example, to weight the scales on the wrong side.

Let us seek to preserve the Christian Sunday because of the things it stands for. Let it be to every Christian a day of honour and delight. All days are the Lord's, but this is pre-eminently His. It comes to us bright with the glory of the resurrection morning, and rich in gracious promises and radiant hopes. Let us make the most of its golden hours and sacred privileges. Not indolence, but worship is its truest rest ; not amusement, but service is its highest joy. Let the fact that it exists for religious ends never be forgotten, and let us resolutely oppose everything that is incompatible with its devotion to these ends. Remember that all we hold dearest is bound up with the sanctity of the Lord's Day.

CHAPTER XIII

JESUS AND HISTORY

WHAT DIFFERENCE HAS JESUS MADE ?

THE other day I was permitted to read a love-letter !
There's something wonderfully thrilling about love-
letters I think—they're often so sad ! And sometimes
they're so sad simply because they're so silly.

However, this love-letter which I was permitted to
read was not the sloppy ' Dearest-Ducky-Darling '
sort of thing—it was just an ordinary sensible letter.
As a matter of fact, it was rather prosaic—and perhaps
its prosaicness was accounted for by the fact that it
was written by a married man. Marriage, they tell
me, sort of takes the gilt off the ginger-bread, so that
married folk soon drop the enthusiastic exuberant
expressions of excessive and ecstatic emotion, and
settle down to act like normal sensible folk.

Well, this fellow had been married long enough to
become normal, and he had been compelled to leave
his wife in their country cottage while he went up to
one of the world's largest cities on business. And they
were expecting in their home that wonderful event
which always makes a big stir in any household—the
advent of a baby. After telling his wife that he was
still in the city, and urging her not to 'fidget' if he had
to stay a little longer, he promised to send her some-

thing as soon as he got his wages, and then proceeded to say an astonishing and amazing thing—writing of the baby, he said : ' *If it is a male, let it live; if it is a female, cast it out.*'

I wonder how that impresses my women readers—the mothers and sisters : ' If it is a male, let it live ; if a female, cast it out.'

Of course the letter was not written by a Britisher ; and it wasn't written recently. As a matter of fact it was written by an Egyptian-Greek nearly two thousand years ago. The letter is dated the year I A.D., and was found on an Egyptian rubbish heap where it had remained buried in the sand for nearly two thousand years.

For the most part it is just an ordinary sort of letter—the sort of thing any husband might write to his wife—sympathetic, masculine, direct and friendly. It is full of trifles, such as greetings to friends and matters of local interest, and then it ends (as we have seen) with that suggestion, inconceivable to us to-day, that if the baby is a girl it need not be kept. It can be put out, either on the land or in the river, and left to kite or crocodile. And the husband didn't see anything unusual or unkind about the suggestion—it was just a common custom.

If such things shock us to-day, it is because two thousand years of Christian teaching have implanted in our hearts a new tenderness, and a respect for human life such as never existed before.

Living, as we do, in an age of cushioned comfort, we are apt to accept many of our privileges without worrying our heads a great deal as to how they came to be. But it is well sometimes, while enjoying our luxury, to pause and ask to whom that luxury is due. To whom is our comfort and all that is good in our modern civilization due ? We owe it to the influence of a Jew, who died on a cross, but whose name is now known as ' the Name above every name.'

But we are going too fast. Let me take you with me on the Magic Carpet of Imagination, back to the year 1 A.D. America, of course, is undiscovered, and the redskins roam the prairies undisturbed. In Britain, where Julius Caesar landed fifty-five years before, the people are for the most part savage—painting their skins (but with different paints from those used by women to-day), hunting their food with bows and arrows, and dancing about around human sacrifices at Stonehenge.

The most important part of the world is round the shores of the Mediterranean Sea. Sticking out into that great inland lake, you remember, is the queer, foot-shaped peninsula, Italy, with, at its centre, Rome—the capital of a vast and wonderful Empire. To the East is Greece, with Athens as the home of Art and culture ; to the far-east, Palestine, with Jerusalem as the home of Monotheistic Religion ; and to the south, Egypt, with Alexandria (founded by Alexander the Great, 332 years before) as the home of philosophy and learning.

We British are so colossally and constitutionally conceited that we are apt to think that there never was a civilization until we started one. That, of course, is not true. As a matter of fact, the Græco-Roman world into which Jesus came was in many ways as astonishing as our own modern world. There were beautiful cities with their libraries, public buildings, theatres and temples. It is true that in rural areas the peasants were crude, and primitive, but in the cities there were architectural triumphs, engineering achievements and intellectual and aesthetic activities which amaze us. In some ways it was a world just like our own—at any rate, it had its war profiteers and its Socialist agitators ; it lamented the decay of the middle classes and even was alarmed over the falling birth rate !

Let me paint you a picture. I need a palette with many pigments, for the picture must be lavish in colour.

A deep blue sky. A white Roman-road made out of great blocks of marble ; by the way-side deep wells of limpid water and the shadowy foliage of spreading plane trees. The road crosses a mountain range. Let us step into the picture and follow it. It leads to the coast with the sea spread out like a great carpet of blue. In the distance is the famous fabled hill Olympus (the home of the gods) the snow on its summit looking like an ethereal dwelling suspended in space. At its foot nestles a city of some 200,000 inhabitants. It is a famous city and has enjoyed a history of increasing prosperity. It rises from the sea fringe in a series of terraces. Through it runs a great highway connecting east with west. By land and by sea it is admirably fitted to be a commercial centre. Sailing in to the harbour travellers find it lovely as a dream. Its white painted walls, its domes and minarets, its groves of cypress, its citadel and its mountain background are enchanting. Such was Thessalonica at the time of Christ. And Thessalonica was typical of many other cities—inwardly prosperous and outwardly beautiful.

But come with me into these cities—get right into them, mix with the people and take part in their activities.   And then the glamour of the beauty fades, and we find at the centre of that ancient civilization, not a spring of clear life giving water, but a stinking cesspool !   Don't shudder at the simile, it is not too strong.   It is no exaggeration to say that that ancient Roman civilization was built over a sewer, its life was polluted at the source.

It has been said that ' ideas rule the world.'   That is true.   ' Thoughts go booming through the world louder than cannon.'   And one's thoughts make one's actions—' as a man thinketh, so is he.'   This is true of civilizations as well as individuals—as they think, so they become.

How did this civilization of two thousand years ago think ?   It thought in terms of superstition.   It was a world teeming with demons and devils, and crammed with creeds and cults.   People to-day seem to be fond of following new religions—but these ancient Romans were almost suffocated with religion—there were so many gods, and minor gods and demons and what-not that it was impossible to count them all.   Their name was legion.   But all these religions were based on either fear or superstitious dread, and had no relation whatever to morality.   Some of them actually encouraged sensuality, in the most degrading forms, as part of their ceremonies.   There were temples dedicated to lust.   Prayer had no moral significance whatever, and was never dedicated to any spiritual ends.   Some of the Roman gods were so debased that no passion was too vile, and no crime too dark to lay before them. A man would pray for the death of a relative that he might inherit his wealth. These pagan Romans would even pray for success in adultery, forgery and theft.

The results of these superstitions, crude creeds and coarse cults can be well imagined. Debased desires make degraded deeds ; and the result was, as one may expect, a civilization that was at its centre as vile and foul as a stinking sewer. So it was that the historian Tacitus wrote : ' I am entering upon the history of a period, rich in disasters, gloomy in wars, rent with seditions, nay, savage in its very hours of peace.' Lust and licence were everywhere. There were adulteries in high places. The seas were crowded with exiles, and the island rocks drenched with murder. Vast regiments of vagrants and beggars lounged near the city gates or haunted the steps and colonades of temples. Everywhere work was regarded with profound disgust as beneath the dignity of free men. Honesty was almost unknown, lying and deceit the usual, instead of the unusual thing, and there were always crowds of folk ready to hire themselves out for every kind of unworthy and degrading task.

Few things lay bare the heart of a nation or an age more surely than its sports. In throwing themselves into these with complete abandon, men reveal the true trend and spirit of their lives.

Tried by this test, the Roman world at the time of Christ presents the saddest of sights. The most popular forms of sport were the gladiatoral shows, for which large buildings were erected—the Colosseum seated some 80,000, and the Circus Maximus some 205,000 spectators. These events were nothing more than scenes of organized carnage, in which the strong odour of saffron was not able to extinguish the still

stronger odour of blood. The gladiators were trained
in special schools where they learnt their strange trade
and bartered their lives for food, pledging themselves
to fight till they fell and be ready to meet the friend
of to-day as the foe of to-morrow. Even women were
trained to fight. There were combats between dwarfs
and blindfolded men. Slaves were led into the arena
naked, unarmed and chained together, to be attacked
by beasts, while their frantic struggles and cries were
gloated over with fiendish delight. It is said that
Tragan, who lived in the first century, on one occasion
brought 10,000 men into the arena in a carnival of
blood which lasted 123 successive days. Under Titus,
5,000 animals perished in a single day, and under
Caligula, 5,000 bears. *Cruelty was a commonplace and
not a crime in that pre-Christian civilization.*

It has been said that ' the key to the difference
between ancient and modern civilizations lies in this
—that the modern civilization aims at the common
weal of the people, while the ancient thought only
of the interests of the favoured few.' That is true.
The population of Rome during the first century of
the Christian Era was 1,610,000, and of that number
900,000 were slaves ! Think of it—three out of five
of the men and women whom Paul passed on the
streets, slaves with less rights, in the eyes of the law,
than my dog ! The law to-day will not permit me
to treat my dog as any Roman slave owner might
treat his slave. Most free men owned them. The
household was beneath consideration which had not
ten. Some of the nobles owned them by tens of
thousands. Five hundred was a common number.

And they were absolutely and entirely at the mercy of their masters. Slavery robbed a man of every right that nature gave him—and the slave woman was little better than an animal.

It is not surprising that in a State so steeped in superstition, sensuousness, and sensuality, that there should be many criminals. In fact, according to our modern standards, almost every person one met could have been classed as such—but the chief offences in those days were those which either directly or indirectly threatened the power of the Emperor. One of the favourite methods of punishment, as you know, was to spread the victim out on a wooden cross like vermin, and leave him to die at his leisure. By and by the crows would gather round the cross, waiting to pick the flesh from the suspended skeleton.

We have already seen, from the letter I quoted you at the beginning of this chapter, how unwanted children were left to die : but I did not tell you that often they would be picked up by a trader in foundlings, who would keep and train them for immoral purposes.

There is just one other thing one ought to mention —and that is the general attitude towards women. Woman to-day is enjoying a liberty such as has never been known in the history of her sex before. She is free. And she stands on an equal footing with men. I wonder how many women stop to think to whom that freedom and equality is really due. Its worth thinking over. Who set the ball rolling ? It was the young Jew—Jesus.

During the spring of 1931 most of us had to put our brains in steep in order to fill up correctly the census papers which were left at every house. We had, you

remember, to record on buff schedules such details
as our sex and occupation, and even our correct
ages ! And this was particularly annoying when one
realized that the head of every household could
discover the exact age of every one living under his
roof ! But if we had been living in the ancient days
of which I've been writing, our women folk would
have been spared the annoying indignity of recording
in black and white their correct ages, for only the
men over twenty counted—women and children didn't
matter. They were simply the property of man who
could do with them pretty much as he liked. He
could even sell them if he chose, like anything else.

Such then was the world into which Jesus came—a
world of superstition and immorality, with little sense
of decency, and little respect for truth or honesty.
A world rent with seditions, a world in which cruelty
was a commonplace and not a crime. A world in which
the chief amusement was torture and bloodshed ; in
which sixty per cent. of its people were slaves with
less rights than a dog, in which criminals were tortured
in a crude and cruel way, in which unwanted children
were left to die or be trained as prostitutes, and a
world in which women were simply the chattels of
men.

Dean Church once said, ' It is a matter of historical
fact that in the closing days of Rome an entirely new
set of moral ideas and moral purposes, of deep
significance, fruitful in consequence, and of a strength
and intensity unknown before, were making their
way into Society, and establishing themselves in it.
It is to the awakening of the new morality, which
has never perished from the hearts of men from that

day to this, that the efforts and successes of modern civilization are mainly due ; it is on the permanence of those moral convictions that it rests. . . . '

And that new moral idealism was due, of course, to the influence of those apostles whom the Jew of Nazareth had sent into the world to preach His Gospel to all nations.

Remembering then, the slavery, the cruelty, the callousness, the cheapness of human life, the indifference to the value of personality, the sensuality, the moral laxity, the absence of honesty and decency, the attitude towards womanhood—aren't you glad you live in the year 1932 and not in the year 2 ?   I am ! I thank God I am privileged to live in an age which knows the music of the word ' mother,' which thinks of woman as the Queen of the Home and not a mere chattel, which reverences personality, values life, and cares for the children as no age has done before.   I am thankful to live in an age which, in spite of its many failings, considers cruelty a crime and not a commonplace.

And I repeat, the difference is due to the teaching and influence of Jesus of Nazareth. By getting down to the source of action—to men's thoughts—Christ has changed the world. He began, as we know, by changing men's ideas of God ; and by giving them new ideas of God he has changed the world. By teaching men that God is Love and no respecter of persons ; by teaching brotherhood and those virtues we now call ' Christian virtues '—virtues such as tolerance, kindness, and honesty—by teaching that only the pure in heart shall see God ; and above all, by showing men how life should be lived, Christ has changed the course of history, and brought to life a new dignity, beauty and charm.

Dr. Jackson once said, ' The thought we make of God is the thought which makes us.' That is true. And by giving the world a new conception of God, Christ gave it new life. The reason why we no longer think of gods as debased and belittled creatures, why we do not believe monstrous and silly superstitions, such as darkened and poisoned the life of Rome, is that Christianity has taught us differently. If we have any thought of God that is pure and loving and tender, if we believe that He cares for all men, and that His love enfolds the weak as well as the strong, the poor as well as the rich, and the folk of every nation ; if when we pray we say ' Father '—it is to Christ we owe it !

Read of what religion means in lands to-day, where the light of the gospel has not shone ; read of life in the redskin wigwam before Egerton Young took the Gospel of Love ; read of life in Labrador before Grenfell took the Gospel of Healing ; read of life in cannibal Calabar before little Mary Slessor took the Gospel of Gentleness—read through the leaves of Missionary biography and history ; then turn to your Bible and read of the nations around Israel in the days of old, read your Old Testament with a pencil in one hand and underline all the stories of cruelty— those stories of the childhood of Israel when she was groping for truth ; and then read your New Testament —turn to St. Luke and read the story of the Prodigal Son, read the prayer Jesus taught his disciples to pray, read of the tender intimacies of the upper room, read the story of the Crucifixion on Calvary's Hill ; reflect upon the significance of that prayer ' Father forgive them '—and you will begin to understand something of the measureless change which Christ has wrought in the world by changing men's thoughts of God. Think, too, of the difference the advent of Christian Missionaries made in Britain, reflect upon the institutions which owed their origin to missionary enterprise, think of the literature, the art, the music, which owes its inspiration to the Christ, and you'll realize something of the difference that He has made.

If you take from Britain all the buildings, the pictures, the books, the poems, the institutions, the philanthropies, the organizations which owe their origin to the influence of Christ, you will have very little left, for almost all we hold dear owes its origin to Him.

It has taken the world a long time to learn His lessons. And even now we do not fully comprehend the full significance of His messages. But we have caught hold of scraps of His ideas—and whenever and wherever men have caught but fragments of His teaching they have worked for the redemption of their fellows. From the simple philosophy of Life taught to a handful of followers by a travelling peasant preacher 1900 years ago, there have sprung, as flowers from seeds, movements which have been inestimable blessings to humanity. In the fullness of time there sprang from His teaching the movement which freed the slave, and there grew from the seed of His thoughts that mighty tree of philanthropy whose branches cover the whole earth, and whose leaves are for the healing of all nations.

There are those who claim a desire to work for the good of humanity, who call themselves altruists and what-not, who profess socialist and humanitarian ideals, but who will admit no allegiance to the Christ. They make me smile. They think themselves clever and original—but they forget they are cultivating flowers from the seed originally sown by Christ. It was He who gave the seed in the first place. As someone has said, ' All that is best in our modern civilization, goes back to Him as its source and fount.'

Do you wonder then that men before us made the coming of Christ the great dividing line of history ? Are you surprised that men decided even to measure time by Him ? Are you surprised that every civilized calendar is reckoned from His Birth ? Do you wonder that every morning all the newspapers in the civilized world readjust their date to His Cradle ? Are you surprised that each New Year as it arrives is baptized with His Name ? That Acts of Parliament, business, politics, literature, the very date upon our cheques and letters are adjusted to the chronology of His Life ? Do you wonder that Paul Richter could say ' the crucified Jew, being the holiest among the Mighty, and the Mightiest among the Holy, had lifted with His pierced hands Empires off their hinges, turned the stream of centuries out of its channel, and still governs the ages ' ?

It is not mere reverent piety to call Jesus ' Lord ' —it is rather the instinctive expression of our deep-rooted consciousness, that with Christ, as never before or since, a new beginning was made and a new era opened !

CHAPTER XIV

JESUS AND US

WHAT IS MY ATTITUDE TOWARDS JESUS?

Do you know that song which goes : ' There ain't no sense, sitting on a fence, all by yourself in the moonlight ? ' Well, that's going to be the ' hook ' on which to hang my last chapter.

It is really surprising what a lot of sound sense there is hidden behind some of our seemingly silly songs. Listen to the song again : ' There ain't no sense, sitting on a fence, all by yourself in the moonlight.' It's a very charming and romantic thing to go ' roamin' in the gloamin' with a lassie by your side,' and to whisper sweet nothings in her pearl-like ears, and then halt, and sitting on a fence become sentimental as you watch the moon rise. And (being a bachelor) I must say that it's often very nice too, to go ' roamin' in the gloamin ' *without* a lassie by your side—to just stroll along in the twilight, and then sit on a fence just lost in thought as the moon casts her spell over you.

But moonlight isn't healthy ! It's apt sometimes to *turn your brain* ! That's how we get the term ' loony,'—from ' luna,' which is Latin for moon : a loony is one whose head has been turned by the moon ! So you see, if moonlight is likely to upset your mental balance, there ' ain't no sense sitting on a fence all by yourself in the moonlight.'

Another thing, fences are often insecure. Once, when I had a party of young folk rambling in the country, some of the girls began to tire and so seated themselves on a fence to rest. There were about twenty of them, and they had hardly got themselves comfortable when the fence broke and precipitated the whole crowd backwards into a bed of nettles ! ! Fences are often insecure, and there isn't any sense in sitting on a fence which is likely to let you down into a bed of nettles !

And yet there are crowds of people who will persist in sitting on fences—metaphorically I mean. They've gone so far, and they'll go no further—they just sit on their fence half way between one thing and another.

Here's one. He's fair, fat and forty ; placid, and comfortably contented. The sort of man who takes a season ticket on the lines of least resistence. The country is faced with a great issue. The newspapers print challenging leading articles, politicians deliver passionate speeches, and ordinary folk like you and me stand at the street corner discussing the situation. It is an issue of vital importance and we must give our vote, and decide ' for ' or ' against.'

But our comfortable friend *refuses to face the problem*. He is not interested in politics, he says. He doesn't care for newspapers and party conflict, he prefers to be neutral. And so he sits on his neutral fence like a solemn old owl blinking in the moonlight, when every one else is trying to decide what is the correct solution to the problem. And it's a problem whose solution may affect his children and grandchildren in scores of vital ways. Are you surprised, then, that the world turns upon him an accusing finger and cries ' There ain't no sense, sittin' on a fence, all by yourself in the moonlight.'

Here's another fence sitter. He's in his early twenties—he's just learnt how to use a razor without cutting himself, smoke a pipe without being sick, and wear a bowler hat at the correct angle. He's very smart looking, but he hasn't much ambition beyond desiring to be a bit of a swell and ' one of the boys ! ' In conversation he never gets much beyond purpose- less prattle of barmaids or turf tipsters, or a discussion as to exact length of a ballet girl's skirt. He's not really bad—but he's not really good. He's not exactly a sinner ; but he's certainly not a saint. He's neither hot nor cold—just lukewarm—he's a *tepid temperament*. In other words, he's sitting on the fence half way between the Kingdom of Heaven, and—the other place!

But, you know, you can't live sitting on a fence, either actually or metaphorically. We live by activity —as soon as you cease to be active you begin to lose the use of your limbs. You try sitting on a fence for a couple of hours, and when you want to get off you'll find yourself so stiff that you can hardly stand : and if you sit long enough you'll become paralysed.

And its just the same in morals. Moral neutrality leads to moral paralysis. I know lots of people who are morally paralysed. They are not definitely immoral, neither are they definitely moral—just half way—sort of moral jellies, sloppy watery wobbly things! They fill me with contempt. I want to live, not wobble through my life ! And you can't live properly, you can't live an abundant life, if you are just content

to sit on a moral fence.   Life is a battle—its not a
thing to be played with and trifled with—its a serious
and strenuous affair.

Here's another fence sitter.   He's often called ' the
man in the street.'   That means he's a creature of
' no man's land ! '   He's not in the Church, neither is
he in prison or in the pub or anywhere else except the
street.   He's neither religious or irreligious.   If there
are Special Services with brief bright brotherly talks
and solos by Miss Jenks, then he'll come and sit in the
gallery and eat monkey nuts or chewing gum.   But
he won't make a stand.   He's non-committal.   He's
just a spectator—sitting on his fence looking first to
one side and then to the other.

He looks on the side labelled Christianity and finds
there's much in the teaching of Jesus he likes and
admires.   But on the other hand, there's a lot that he
doesn't like because it's hard, and so he turns round and
looks to the other side of his fence—the side labelled
' Indifference.'   This side certainly looks more comfortable and entrancing.   There's a ruggedness and a
hardness about the other side which fills him with awe.
There's a restfulness about the indifference side
which gives to him a feeling of tranquillity.   Then
again, there's mystery too—on the other side—things
he can't explain and understand.

He doesn't mind accepting Jesus as a human teacher
who set a good example, but all the stuff about
divinity and miracles and so on—it puzzles him, it
means he must do a bit of hard thinking, and he's too
lazy to think.   So he wobbles about on his fence like
a parrot wobbling from side to side on its perch—
cocking its head first to one side and then the other—

trying to look wise but really looking so absurd that he becomes a laughing stock and source of entertainment.

But you can't wobble about like that indefinitely. To change to metaphor, you must look one way or the other—you can't go through life with a spiritual squint ! You can't be conscientious objectors and shirk your obligations in matters of religion and morals. There's a challenge—and you must choose or reject.

> Passionately fierce the voice of God is pleading,
>   Pleading with men to arm them for the fight ;
> See how those hands, majestically bleeding,
>   Call us to rout the armies of the night !

So you see the song rings true. ' There ain't no sense, sitting on a fence, all by yourself in the moonlight.' To put it into modern slang—it's balmy to sit on a fence ; and God never intended us to be balmy— He intended us to be brave. He never intended us to make silly fools of ourselves—but He did intend us to be fighters.

Now let's suppose that you are sitting on a fence, and intend to remain there. What then ? I'm speaking of the moral fence now. Here you are—a neutral, not definitely good, not definitely bad—just half way. And as you sit on your neutral fence there comes the King of kings challenging you to conflict on the side of truth and beauty and purity. You disregard the challenge.

Then comes the King of the other Kingdom—and he's beautifully disguised. Satan in satin sort of thing ; he's ' dressed in his best, and it's all for you,' and he's laden with presents, and passionately he

whispers promises to you. You stoop to listen to
those honey'd suggestions—and you lose your balance
—and over the fence you go—and you land on the
wrong side—deep, deep in nettles ! The language of
course is figurative—but that's just what happens—
I've seen it over and over again. Moral wobbling
usually ends in beggary of body and soul.

I can think of men who went to school with me who
have wrecked their own lives and broken their parents'
hearts because they were moral wobblers. I can think
of fellows who were apprentices with me who have
ruined their careers, wasted their opportunities and
ended in beggary of body and soul because they hadn't
the pluck to make a stand.

A young man was one day talking to the pilot of a
large American river steamer.

' How long,' he asked, ' have you been a pilot on
these waters ? '

' Twenty-five years,' the old man replied.

' Then,' said the young man, ' I should think
you must know every rock and sand bank on the
river.'

The old man smiled at the youth's simplicity, and
replied, ' Oh, no, I don't ; but I know where the deep
water is.'

He wasn't taking risks in the shallows—that was
asking for trouble—and he kept to the deep waters.

Now, you know where the deep water is on the
river of life as well as I do—and if you've any sense
at all you'll get there and keep there. You wouldn't
sit smoking fags on the top of a powder magazine.
You wouldn't sit wobbling on a fence if on one side
of it there were a precipice. Well, there's a precipice

on the one side of the moral fence—but it's so skilfully covered that many don't know it's there till they tumble over it. Don't forget—the fence is there to keep you on the right side—not to sit on.

Suppose we were all to sit on the fence! What then? Supposing all those who are definitely fighting for the right were suddenly to climb on a fence and say, ' We're not going to carry on with this fighting business any longer—we're going to let men go hang—if they want to go to the Devil, let 'em go, and may they jolly well enjoy his company ! '

What would happen then? I'll tell you. It would mean that in a very short time our civilization would stagger unsteadily into a cesspool of undiluted cruelty and filth ; and sink and sink, until at last there would be no course left but to be submerged—submerged in the stink and slime of it all.

' Oh,' you say, ' on what have you to found such a statement ?'

I'll tell you.

There are in Europe at present a larger number of men and women who are opposed to Christianity and its moral teaching than there have been for many generations. Just listen to what some of these people say and write.

First, they say, the world is over-populated ; there are too many of us, and the only remedy is to have some of us killed off ! In order to do that we must recognize as legal and moral, not merely the prevention of birth, but ' infanticide ' (that is, infant murder) as well ! Every mother and father must be left free to decide which of their new born babies they shall kill and which they shall keep alive.

Secondly, the whole of our civilization is based upon a fallacy. Christianity has made men sentimental, and what the world needs is to rid itself of all the tosh preached in churches, and free itself of the silly restriction of society. Man, these people say, is just an animal, who through an evolutionary process happens to have had its brain specially developed ; and once we realize this fact, and start to live natural animal lives, all the troubles of our artificial civilization will pass away. Set men and women perfectly free from restrictions, and they will be as innocent and unconscious of wrong as dogs and cats, and they will strangle their babies with tender hearts.

All you have to do is to get rid of the men in the queer collars, turn your churches into cabaret shows, teach children that they are just highly developed animals, give youth all the hot-house thrills and pleasures it wants, and let lust burn as brightly as it will.

Once you have converted people to this point of view, they will realize that our present marriage laws are out-of-date and simply based on silly sentiment ; if we can get rid of the sentiment, and look at the question in a sane and scientific way, we shall realize that it is perfectly obvious half a husband is better than no husband at all, and that the problem of the unwanted woman and the White Slave Traffic can be easily solved by legalizing ' free love ' or arranging for marriages of a limited duration. If you can somehow or other kill off the ministers of Christianity, men will then be free to live according to the new creed.

There you are ! That's the alternative of Christianity—stark naked and stripped of all its disguise.

And I'm not making it up—the ideas I have just outlined are seriously taught by a certain school of teachers to-day. You can read it up for yourself. Sometimes it is doled out in as stark and ugly a way as I've given it, sometimes it comes to us dressed up in its Sunday clothes masquerading as novels or psychology—but it's there—being circulated among the children of this generation, trying to lure us back to the jungle.

And lots of folk who call themselves ' highbrows ' and want to appear clever, just drink it in as a baby drinks its milk, and then when they've fattened themselves on it come into the world and tell us they've found a new gospel.

And my own idea is this—It's all founded on a preposterous lie ! It is true that man is an animal—but he is not just an animal. Can the most intelligent animal you have ever seen or heard of, write a sonnet, or sail a ship, compose a sonata or cultivate seeds, paint a picture or make a plum pudding, write a poem or make pastry, solve a problem in algebra or build a bridge, stage a play or sing a hymn, play polo or pray ?

Apart from its physical characteristics, has your intelligent animal anything you can really compare with humanity ? It can run, but can it regret ? It can walk, but can it wonder ? It can fight, but can it forgive ? It can be affectionate, like your dog, but can it aspire, like your daughter.

And suppose we do begin strangling our babies—would that be progression ? I should call it ' retrogression.' They used to do that 2,000 years ago in the days when our savage ancestors were dancing about in animal skins and knocking sense into their wives with clubs !

Supposing we do return to the freedom and innocency of the animals, doesn't it follow that we shall return to their brutality too ?   I say the doctrine is founded on a lie, and it makes life a mean scramble for passion and pleasure, with no real value, no real romance, and no heroism.   It's just a sordid struggle for self-satisfaction.   There have been thousands who have lived that kind of life throughout the centuries— with no sense of shame and no attempt at restraint— and they've been pretty rotten advertisements of their doctrine too.   What they have done is this—they have kidded themselves up that there is no such thing as sin, and then they've taken their own sins and dressed them up in the robes of these wonderful doctrines— and then knelt down and worshipped them.

And if we were to take these people seriously, and follow their direction, it would mean that our civilization would plunge head first into the cesspool—life would become cheap—lust would be legal.   Every man would be a law unto himself, as they were on the American prairies 100 years ago—with the same disastrous results.   Freedom would become licence, murder would be common and condoned, human life would be cheap, home life would disappear, children would be left to drift, idealism would go—and—why, bless my soul, its too terrible to think what that ' and ' would imply. The world has seen Babylon, Bysantium and Rome let go their ideals and integrity and plunge head first into the cesspool of lewdness and filth and cruelty until they were eventually submerged and rotted in their own rottenness ; and if Europe were to let go in a similar way, it would mean Paradise would be lost for ever and all Hell let loose.

That idea that if you set all men free from restraint and the fetters of convention they will become moderate and innocent and decent people, has about as little evidence to rest on as any lie I know.

I am free to play a violin, and when I do I am bound by no laws and subject to no conventions, and the result is—I produce the most terrible and ear-splitting squeals and scratches it is possible to imagine ! The real musician is one who obeys—he is a slave, bound by laws and conventions ; but he produces music that brings tears to the eyes and which the angels must sometimes stoop to hear.

And if a man is to make music of life, if his life is to be a harmony and not a discord, he must be bound by the laws of the master musician and must be subject to the conventions of Society and the commands of Christ.

And so, it resolves itself into this—life is really a great choice—a choice between religion and rottenness, Christ and chaos. For my part—I choose the Christ and give myself to fight unreservedly on His side.

> So would I live and not in idle resting,
>   Stupid as swine that wallow in the mire ;
> Fain would I fight, and be for ever breasting
>   Danger and death, for ever under fire !

Now what about you ? You've read my book, you've probably listened to scores of sermons—have you made the choice ? Or are you still on the fence ? If so, I want to urge you to leave it—to set out to find the Holy Grail of Spotless Manhood or Womanhood according to the pattern wrought by Jesus. Leave

the dirt and the smut, the lies and the meanness—
leave them behind you because they are so beastly
ugly, and follow the Christ in all His purity and beauty.

Do you know of anything better for a man than to
be like Christ ?   I don't.   One of the bravest soldiers
of the Great War said, ' You may say you know of a
better ideal, then for God's sake fork it out.   I don't.
I never came across any one in history who could
pretend to stand in the same street with Him.'

And Stanley Jones in his quiet and cultured way
says : ' I know of nothing better for a man than to
be Christlike.   The highest adjective descriptive of
character in any language is Christlike.   No higher
compliment can be paid to a man than to be called
Christlike.'

Let me lead you once more through Gethsemane
on to Calvary into the shadow of the cross.   There it
looms above the world—and beneath it the great
common crowd surges beneath the sweltering sun.
And on the cross there hangs the tortured figure of the
Christ.   And He has hung there for two thousand years.
There is still a Calvary in the heart of God.   Man still
takes goodness and crucifies it, he still takes purity and
spits on it.   They used to tell me that God arranged
that cross.   I don't believe it.   God didn't arrange
that gory mess.   Man arranged that !   What God
arranged was a caress.   He wanted to draw all men to
His great Heart of Love :   but the caress was refused,
and the result was a cross.   The cross of Calvary was
only the material symbol of the cross in God's heart.

And I have brought you into the shadow of that
cross again, because it is God's challenge to you—it
is a challenge to all of us to take up the struggle of

the higher life, to bear its burden and endure its shame and win its inward peace.

I began the chapter with the words of a comic song, I end with a familiar text of Scripture—' Choose you this day whom ye will serve.' Will you close the book, and kneel in imagination at the foot of Calvary, and pray this prayer:

> Bread of Thy body give me for my fighting,
>   Give me to drink Thy sacred Blood for wine,
> While there are wrongs that need me for the righting,
>   While there is warfare splendid and divine.
>   Give me for light, the sunshine of Thy sorrows,
>   Give me for shelter, the shadow of Thy Cross.

EPILOGUE

Now I must bring my little book to an end. I have tried to grapple, in a free and easy way, with some of the questions which men and women are asking every day. I cannot pretend to be able to give final and dogmatic answers to all these questions, there are no final certainties : only tremendous probabilities.

I've been puzzling over problems ever since I can remember : but I never reach final solutions to my problems. Often I have found myself arguing in a circle—covering the same ground over and over again, and not realizing that it *was* the same ground because of the ' encircling gloom.' But always my arguments bring me back to one place (and no matter which way I travel, the ultimate destination is always the same). That place is Calvary. Somehow or other I cannot get away from there—the Cross seems to be interwoven into the very fibre of the Universe.

We all admit that the Universe is a mystery. But the greatest Mystery of all, to my mind, is a crucified Christ becoming a *conquering* Christ ! Perhaps that's why He fascinates us so much. We begin by pondering over a mystery, and end by being impressed by a Majesty. And the more we think of Him, the more we feel that it is not so much His Mystery which fascinates, as His Majesty which awes ! Someone has said : ' Take hold of Jesus as a man, and you will discover Him as God.'

The very fact that the newspapers of five continents, and most of the millions of letters which are written every day by people of every country, are dated from the birth of a Jew who was crucified nearly two thousand years ago, is tremendously significant ! Why don't we date our letters and papers from the time of Caesar, or Augustus, or Alexander, or Napoleon, or any other great personality of history ? Why give the honour to an obscure carpenter who died in disgrace on a criminal's cross ? Why not give it to a prince instead of a peasant ? And why a Jew—a member of that despised little race ? Why measure time from Him ?

The answer seems to be because we cannot get away from Him ! He *is* the centre of history—history revolves around Him. Even before His birth He was dreamed of, and prophesied, and expected. And now, two thousand years after His death, He is still talked of in nearly every corner of the world ! There have been millions upon millions who have lived and died since the dawn of history, but only One who died and *still lives* !

Some years ago, Tennyson, in his ' Children's Hospital ' made a doctor say :

' All very well—but the good Lord Jesus has had His day.'

And a nurse replied : ' Had ? Has it come ? It has only dawned. It will come by and by.'

There are still those who suggest that the good Lord Jesus has had His day. (Perhaps there are more of these pessimistic prophets now than there were in Tennyson's day.) But in spite of them the good Lord Jesus still captivates the hearts of men, awes their spirits and baffles their intellects.

Tennyson's nurse said : ' O, how could I serve in the wards if the hope of the world were a lie ? '

And there are some of us to-day who would say : ' How could we do anything really worth while if the hope of the world were a lie ? ' If I couldn't believe in Christ and God I think I'd go mad—I should certainly ' go the pace,' because there'd be nothing to hold me off the ' line of least resistance.' It's hard enough to keep straight as it is, and one often slips and stumbles on the way.

The other day two kiddies persisted in holding my hands and dragging me to the top of a hill with the sole purpose of running me down again ! And we repeated the performance till we were utterly exhausted. I'm afraid much of our human effort is like that ! We climb—up and up, so slowly and laboriously—and then, like Jack and Jill, we come tumbling down to the bottom, only to start all over again ! But if the hope of the world were a lie who'd bother to climb up again ? Not I. I think I know myself well enough to know that I'd stay down and proceed to enjoy wallowing in the muck ! To change the metaphor, I'd get the bit between my teeth, and closing my eyes gallop helter skelter straight for Hell !—I'd saturate myself in sin and sordidness, because, once I really let go, I couldn't hold myself back. It's my belief in God which holds me back ! And I believe in God because I believe in Jesus. I can't understand many of the mysteries of life, I can't answer many of the questions of life, I find it difficult to believe in a Being whom I cannot see—to believe in the invisible, intangible, incomprehensible power which created and controls the universe, and which we English folk call 'GOD.' I find it difficult to believe that insignificant little creatures like men can have a place in the thoughts of such a Creator. It is difficult for me to believe that a mere man can have communion with such a Being. It is hard sometimes to think of that Being as kind, when Nature seems so cruel. It is hard to believe in a great purpose running through history when one thinks of such horrors as wars like the Great War. To me, life is full of intellectual difficulties. But the greatest difficulty of all is to get away from Jesus.

I can't get away from Him. He is inescapable. I have tried to escape Him—tried to escape Him more than I've tried to escape anything else in life. I have tried to explain Him away. I have tried to forget Him, to live without Him. But I can't. It's the story of the Hound of Heaven again!

> I fled Him down the nights and down the days . . .
>   But with steady unhurrying chase . . .
>   Came on the following Feet,
>   And a Voice above their beat—
> 'Naught shelters thee, who wilt not shelter Me.'

Whichever way I have turned I have sooner or later found Him following. It has been uncanny, almost terrifying. Once I was told that historians could explain Him away. So I turned to History—and I found two thousand years writ large with His Name. Jesus is fact, historical fact. He was such a real fact in the days of his flesh that He remains fact now. Some fifty years or so before Him there lived one Julius Caesar—a soldier, a scholar, a man of many parts. But Caesar died—and remained dead, as dead as Cleopatra or King Charles. Jesus Christ died, and yet He still lives. When a school boy I had to translate some of Caesar's writings and learn dull dates about him. Most Secondary-school boys have to translate Caesar's 'Wars.' But Caesar means nothing to them. Men don't wrangle, argue and fight, suffer, sacrifice and do all manner of heroic deeds for the love of Julius Caesar. But they do for the love of Jesus Christ. There's the difference.

There's something about Jesus which is unique. He is inescapable and inexplicable. He baffles our intellects and awes our spirits. I begin by finding myself compelled to accept Him as a man—a historical figure. But I soon find myself worshipping Him as God. And I don't want to ! I don't want to, because there are so many intellectual snags in the way. I don't quite know what I mean by 'divinity.' And I find myself mystified by the term ' Trinity.' I want to know how a God can ' empty Himself ' and where God was when Jesus hung on the cross—and hosts of other things. But I'm driven to it. Like that doubting disciple of old, I can only prostrate myself in wonder and cry ' My Lord and my God.'

You see, it's not so much a matter of argument as of choice. It isn't so much a matter of answering questions as of accepting an invitation.

One voice says, ' Here is the secret of happy and successful living.' But another voice says, ' It is not there—it is here, this is the Way, stop questioning and follow.'

And I ask, ' How ? What must I do ? '

The Voice replies, ' Sell all.'

But I ask, ' What does that mean ? Does it mean sell all my material possessions ? '

' Sometimes it means that,' the Voice replies, ' but always it means renounce self.'

I reply, ' There are other questions I have to ask. What about . . .'

And the Voice interrupts, ' You must simply " let go "—sell all ; you must even be willing to let go your questionings, they are some of the things you are still clinging to. Sell all—and the pearl of great price is yours.'

Then I just trust—and the pearl is mine, gloriously mine !

It's taken me many years to learn this simple truth. But now I am convinced that it is the only thing to do. Just let go. Jesus does not ask us to explain Him, or even try to understand Him. He just challenges us to be plucky enough to follow.

And when we do let go we find to our delight and sometimes our surprise, that we have become possessors of treasures which change the whole of life. Old things pass away and all things become new. And in our new joy we find ourselves sharing the experience of those great saints of the Methodist Revival who could sing, and mean what they sang :

> In the heavenly Lamb
> Thrice happy I am,
> And my heart it doth dance at the sound of His name.

Sometimes, I think, we try to make ourselves believe that we cannot accept God through Jesus because of our intellectual difficulties, when in reality we are just building walls around ourselves because we are afraid of the inexorable demands Jesus makes. Very often it is fear which is holding us back when we pretend it is our questionings. More often than not we are afraid, afraid to give up our sins, afraid of what our friends will think or say if we try to live a new life, afraid, perhaps, of becoming more than we dare to be. But to gain the pearl we must sell all. Let everything go and just hold on to Jesus.

> Oh make but trial of his love,
> Experience will decide.

In a little collection of real religious experiences called *A Group Speaks*, a young lady who calls herself Irene, says this :

' I was thoroughly unhappy. I used to dread going to chapel ; but I daren't stay away, partly because I was afraid I should miss what I was seeking, and partly because mother and father would have wanted to know why. I remember one service in particular. The sermon was on the foundations of our faith—building on the rock. I don't think I have ever felt more miserable in a service before or since. The closing hymn was 362 :

> Now I have found the ground wherein
> Sure my soul's anchor may remain.

' I stood silent—I couldn't sing that hymn, and I wanted to. Two Sundays later the text was the single word " COME." I heard Jesus saying that, and, well—I loved Him so much I just had to go to Him. I knew there were difficulties still unsolved, but somehow they had ceased to matter. Jesus and I would face them together. And if I had to wait for a solution, I didn't mind. I had Him, and nothing else mattered.'

I want to leave you there, reader. You too, perhaps, have problems still unsolved. But if you would enter into the full experience of the life of God and find life full and rich and glorious, you must respond to that invitation ' COME.'

' Come unto Me, and I will give you rest.'

Such is my Faith, and such
My reasons for it, and I find them strong
Enough. And you ? You want to argue ? Well,
I can't. It's a choice. I choose the Christ.